HELP
ME HELP
OTHERS

HELP ME HELP OTHERS

*Practical Ways to Build
Healthy Relationships*

LARRY R. WAGNER, Ph.D.

REDEMPTION
PRESS

Published by Redemption Press, PO Box 427, Enumclaw, WA 98022
Toll Free (844) 2REDEEM (273-3336)

Redemption Press is honored to present this title in partnership with the author. The views expressed or implied in this work are those of the author. Redemption Press provides our imprint seal representing design excellence, creative content and high quality production.

All Scripture quotations, unless otherwise indicated, are taken from the Holy Bible, New International Version®, NIV®. Copyright ©1973, 1978, 1984, 2011 by Biblica, Inc.™ Used by permission of Zondervan. All rights reserved worldwide. www.zondervan.com The "NIV" and "New International Version" are trademarks registered in the United States Patent and Trademark Office by Biblica, Inc.™

ISBN 13: 978-1-63232-692-8 (SC)
          978-1-63232-738-3 (HC)
          978-1-63232-693-5 (ePub)
          978-1-63232-698-0 (Mobi)

Library of Congress Catalog Card Number: 2015954894

CONTENTS

ACKNOWLEDGMENTS ℰ

The birth of *Help Me Help Others* has finally come after a twenty-year gestation period. Such a lengthy project benefits from the support of many people. I am grateful to the Columbia International University (CIU) community and its president, Bill Jones, for providing me with the privilege of teaching the most dedicated students you will find in any higher educational setting. Their commitment to advancing the kingdom of God is unparalleled. My nineteen-year tenure in the classroom proved to be a fertile environment in which to test and refine the concepts in this book. My colleagues at CIU continue to be a source of great support.

In addition to the academic arena, my church home, Gateway Baptist Church, solidified my belief that there are many caring people in the Body of Christ who are eager to receive practical tools with which to engage those who are hurting. Thank you to all those wounded healers who eagerly grasped the materials in this book and have used them to make a difference in the lives of others. This would not have been possible without the support of Don Brock, Ronald Flynn, and the other leaders in the church.

I am humbled by and indebted to the men and women who have entrusted me with their personal stories. With names being changed, I have included a few of those stories to help the reader see how to apply the *Help Me Help Others* concepts in the context of a caring relationship.

At the risk of excluding some key people, there are a few who deserve special recognition. Thank you to Kristine Steakley, Glenn Stanton, and Loretta Goddard for reading earlier drafts and providing helpful and encouraging feedback. Many thanks are due to the team at Redemption Press for their support and professionalism. My dear friends and accountability partners, David Olshine and Hule Goddard were with me from the beginning of this project and have tirelessly prayed with me through its completion. Thank you David and Alice, Daphne and Steve, and John for the physical, emotional, and spiritual support you provided during my bone marrow transplant and in my ongoing battle with MDS.

Ben and Dana, thank you for your willingness to listen and for your insightful feedback as I shared my many musings with you. You fill my heart with joy and pride. I am blessed with an amazing wife whose laughter, patience, compassion, Christ-likeness and many other positive qualities have filled our thirty-seven-year relationship with more enjoyment than I could have ever imagined.

INTRODUCTION —HELP IS ON THE WAY

"The Sovereign LORD has given me a well-instructed tongue, to know the word that sustains the weary. He wakens me morning by morning, wakens my ear to listen like one being instructed" (Isaiah 50:4). I have found few things in life more fulfilling than providing words of encouragement and hope to those who are weary. Isaiah understood that the source of these life-changing words must always be the Sovereign Lord. This verse provides an important reminder that listening to God must precede talking to others.

In an information-saturated world, a simple call or click creates access to vast amounts of relationship advice. There is one drawback. How do we know which advice we can trust? "There is a way that seems right to a man, but in the end it leads to death" (Proverbs 14:12). Have you ever considered the cost of bad advice? A young adult is encouraged by friends to pursue a relationship that should have been avoided. A married couple with a history of conflict is advised to throw in the towel when, with the proper help, they could have developed an amazing partnership. Well-intentioned presenters at a marriage conference offer simplistic solutions to complex problems, thus setting couples up for a post-weekend crash, feelings of despondency, and the conclusion that their relationship is beyond repair. Even trained professionals are at risk for causing significant harm when they offer advice after hearing only one side of the story. Maybe this is what James, the leader of the early church, had in mind when he wrote, "Not many of you should presume to be teachers, my brothers, because you know that we who teach will be judged more strictly" (James 3:1). A modern-day paraphrase might read, "If you are going to offer people advice about how to live, expect to be held accountable for whether it helped."

People come to us in pain, they want relief, and we want to help. How do we decide what kind of help to offer? I am wary of caregivers who offer a one-size-fits-all approach. They suggest that problems can be cured by following their prescribed "to-do" list. A much more respectful approach is to embrace people in their pain and to begin identifying its source. Is it self-inflicted, a result of harm done by others, or an invitation for deeper growth? It is important to consider the third possibility because one of the most damaging beliefs in Christian counseling is to assume that if someone is in pain, they must be out of favor with God. Both the Bible and church history provide numerous examples of God using mild discomfort all the way to severe distress as a precursor for deep personal and spiritual growth. Unfortunately, often due to misguided teachings, people don't allow pain to guide them to deeper truths about themselves or to receive God's comfort because they falsely believe that he should never have allowed them to suffer.

This book was written for compassionate individuals who want to become better equipped to help people who are struggling in their relationships. The practical tools you are about to receive were developed and refined over thirty-five years and many thousands of hours spent listening and responding to people facing relationship challenges. I am grateful for their willingness to include me in their healing process. I am also deeply indebted to my marital lab partner for our thirty-seven year ongoing dialogue. As a patient listener, provider of feedback, and pursuer of God's love and truth, Sue has enriched my life in ways that words cannot capture.

A final word of caution is warranted for those who are looking for quick-fix formulas; this book will not be very satisfying. If, on the other hand, you are interested in learning how to help individuals explore the deeper issues of their heart and how to embrace God's design for relationships, you will find some valuable resources.

You will notice that each major relationship concept is presented with a diagram. The diagrams provide a concrete way to discuss and apply the relationship principles. My hope is that they are profound in both their relevance and simplicity. Feedback from clients and students suggests that the concepts presented in the diagrams are not limited by age, gender, education, or culture. I trust that with the Holy Spirit's guidance you will know the deep satisfaction of using these diagrams and concepts to help hurting people put into words what was previously a jumbled mix of thoughts and emotions. In fact, the concepts used in this book have a language of their own. Terms such as Plugs, Inner Room, Living Sacrifice, Critical Pause, and Forgiveness Marker will provide you and the people you help with a common language for describing the healing, restorative process you share. May you be filled with mercy and grace as you move forward in your eternally-significant endeavor to connect with those who need your help.

Chapter 1

PLUGS

J esus announced the start of his redemptive work on earth by saying, "The time has come ..." (Mark 1:15). For centuries there had been talk about this day and now it had arrived. From this point forward, everyone who heard about the Messiah Jesus would have to make a choice: to believe in him or to reject him.

With his next words, "The kingdom of God has come near," Jesus announced that God's reign would now be established in the hearts of those who believed in him (see Mark 1:15). We no longer have to remain in the grip and under the reign of a sin nature. We can be set free to live as God intended. The life God intended begins each day with an invitation to be loved, to live by the truths found in the Bible, to invest in things of eternal significance, and to maintain a focus on others and especially on those who are suffering. The main purpose of this book is to help you help others live this kind of life.

Jesus concluded his inaugural announcement with the words, "... Repent and believe the good news!" (Mark 1:15). Jesus made it clear from the start that he was not an add-on to life, but the starting point for a life of total surrender.

The good news of God's redemptive plan needed to be shared and explained, so after his announcement, "Jesus went throughout Galilee, teaching in their synagogues, proclaiming the good news of the kingdom, and healing every disease and sickness among the people" (Matt. 4:23). Then, as now, hurting people were struggling to make life work. Jesus responded to their needs by presenting life-changing truths and offering powerful expressions of compassion. In one of his last conversations with his disciples before returning to heaven Jesus said, "… As the Father has sent me, I am sending you" (John 20:21). For those who care to notice, hurting people are still searching for life-changing truths and are waiting for powerful expressions of compassion. Like those disciples of long ago, Jesus is calling us, his modern day disciples, to replicate his example.

There is something unsettling about being asked to emulate someone who in his time of greatest need was abandoned by his friends and then crucified! To truly emulate him, we will need to see people the way Jesus sees them. This will require the ability to see what is not seen. Perhaps this is why Jesus ended so many of his talks with a reminder that the true meaning of his teachings could only be grasped by those who had spiritual eyes and ears. It is as if Jesus wanted his followers to realize that what they saw only represented a small fraction of what was taking place in the world around them. There is a spiritual realm and created order of which this world only gives us a faint glimpse.

Jesus made it clear that the primary implication of living with two co-existing worlds—one material and one spiritual—is that we must choose between them. "No one can serve two masters. Either you will hate the one and love the other, or you will be devoted to the one and despise the other" (Matt. 6:24). The kingdom of the world and the kingdom of God are in direct competition. James, a leader of the early church, described the competition this way, "You adulterous people, don't you know that friendship with the world means enmity against God? Therefore, anyone who chooses to be a friend of the world becomes an enemy of God" (James 4:4). The lines are drawn and choices are required. The competition is fierce because of what is at stake. Will we pursue what this world has to offer as our ultimate goal or will we hunger to see God's kingdom ways done "… on earth as it is in heaven" (Matt. 6:10)?

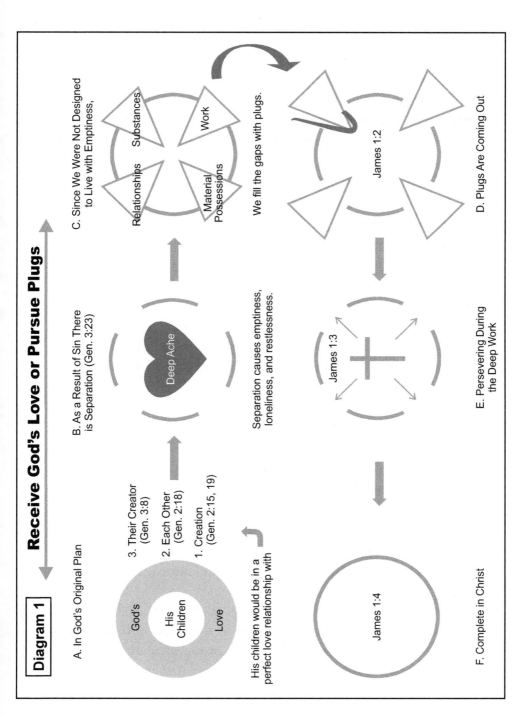

Diagram 1

Receive God's Love or Pursue Plugs

A. In God's Original Plan

God's
His Children
Love

His children would be in a perfect love relationship with

1. Creation (Gen. 2:15, 19)
2. Each Other (Gen. 2:18)
3. Their Creator (Gen. 3:8)

B. As a Result of Sin There is Separation (Gen. 3:23)

Deep Ache

Separation causes emptiness, loneliness, and restlessness.

C. Since We Were Not Designed to Live with Emptiness,

Substances
Work
Relationships
Material Possessions

We fill the gaps with plugs.

James 1:2

D. Plugs Are Coming Out

James 1:3

E. Persevering During the Deep Work

James 1:4

F. Complete in Christ

15

One of the best services we can provide others is to help them clearly see what the different kingdoms offer and to be available with outstretched arms if and when their choices do harm. If we identify ourselves as Christ followers, then our approach to helping people will be similar to his. Specifically, we will present the kingdom truths found in the word of God to hurting people, in the context of a loving relationship, under the full influence of the Holy Spirit.

Diagram # 1 is the first of several diagrams provided in this book to help you help others in a manner consistent with Jesus' model. It is a great place to start your counseling because it begins with God's original design for his creation, explains what happens when we live outside the design, and provides a hopeful look at how God restores us. This diagram also offers a big-picture perspective of what will take place in counseling, which can be very reassuring to those who need to see a plan of action and for those who are leery of the counseling process. As you guide individuals through the six conditions shown in the diagram, they will begin to:

- Grasp God's desire for a personal relationship (Condition A).
- Realize what sin does to cause separation (Condition B).
- Identify current solutions and evaluate how well they are working (Condition C).
- Explore how God lovingly intervenes (Condition D).
- Accept that the most important work will require a change of heart (Condition E).
- Grow into a place of completeness in Christ (Condition F).

Each condition provides an opportunity for dialogue with individuals about what is not working in their lives, a realization of why it is not working, and a specific plan for what can be done to change. The pace for going through the conditions will vary from person to person. I suggest doing a big picture overview of Diagram

1, and then going back and spending as much time as needed on the specific conditions.

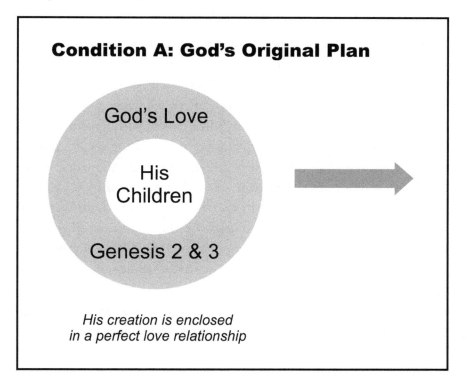

Condition A: God's Original Plan

God's Love

His
Children

Genesis 2 & 3

*His creation is enclosed
in a perfect love relationship*

The best way to understand the heart of the Creator is to examine his creation. At the very foundation of God's creation is the idea of relationship. In the first three chapters of Genesis we gain a glimpse of Father, Son, and Spirit expressing intimacy through a design that included a perfect love relationship:

1. with Creation, which provided Adam with a sense of purpose and freedom as caretaker of the garden and the one who named the animals (Genesis 2:15, 19-20)
2. between Man and Woman, which provided Adam and Eve with emotional connection and enjoyment of each other (Genesis 2:18; 20b-23)

3. with the Creator, which provided Adam and Eve with the opportunity to walk and talk with God "in the cool of the day" about the intricacies of his design (Genesis 3:8)

Mike was a likeable guy who was spiritually and emotionally bankrupt. His journey of faith began in a church he described as friendly toward kids. Some of his best childhood memories came from the summer camps and special programs he attended while at this church. After his parents divorced, however, Mike moved with his mother and two younger siblings across town and began attending what he called an angry church. The junior high school years were the worst of his life. During these years his image of God was shaped by an earthly father who abandoned him and by a heavenly father who, his church told him, was constantly disappointed with him. Mike's college years were marked by a time of searching that fluctuated between weekend fraternity parties and conversations with the leader of a Christian organization on campus.

When Mike came to see me for counseling there was little in his life that reflected the Creator's original plan for perfect love relationships. In the five years since college he had tried three different jobs and felt as clueless as ever about his purpose in life. He was in his second serious relationship with several false starts mixed in. God seemed as distant as ever. Out of a sense of desperation Mike was motivated to search for some answers. Deep down he sensed that his unresolved issues with God were at the core of what was missing.

Mike's life provides an example of the human dilemma. He knew his life was missing something, but he could not find a remedy because he did not yet understand the cause of the problem.

Pause to Consider

What did Mike need from our first few meetings? It may seem obvious, but the first step in helping Mike was to become interested in his story. By carefully listening to his story and enjoying him as the storyteller, I was able to establish a connection with Mike. In an atmosphere where he felt heard, accepted, and even enjoyed, Mike found himself talking about things he had never shared with anyone.

My challenge was to determine how much of his story I needed to hear. Too much and we could get bogged down. Too little and Mike may not feel like I understood. A helpful guideline to follow is to get as much of the story as is needed to begin seeing some reoccurring themes or patterns. At most of the critical junctures in Mike's story, a "disappointment" theme stood out. By following the disappointment theme as we worked through Diagram 1, Mike was able to recognize the source of his disappointment and why his attempts to make it go away (plugs) were unsuccessful.

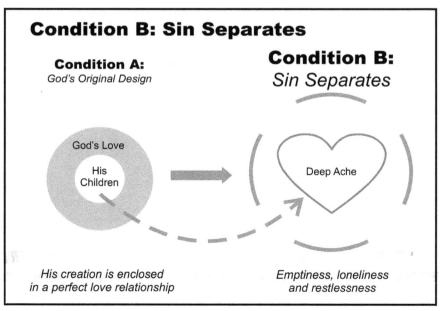

Condition B: Sin Separates

Condition A:
God's Original Design

Condition B:
Sin Separates

God's Love

His Children

Deep Ache

His creation is enclosed in a perfect love relationship

Emptiness, loneliness and restlessness

God created us in perfect love, and then, out of that same love, gave us the choice to receive the offer of relationship on God's terms or to question whether he could be trusted. When Adam and Eve chose not to trust God's love, sin entered their lives and did what it does best: created a separation between them and God. Since then everything in God's creation has felt the effect of living in a way it was not created to live. Paul describes this condition with these words: "We know that the whole creation has been groaning as in the pains of childbirth right up to the present time" (Rom. 8:22).

I explained this to Mike by taking the inner circle (His Children) of Condition A and moving it to Condition B. Separated from God's original design of a perfect love relationship, His children become broken and empty. With a look of frustration Mike said, "I'm not sure whether I'm more frustrated at God for creating his plan this way, or for what sin has done to steal it from me." Other words used by clients to describe Condition B include loneliness, restlessness, emptiness, darkness, and despair. Mike and I summarized it as a deep ache in the heart.

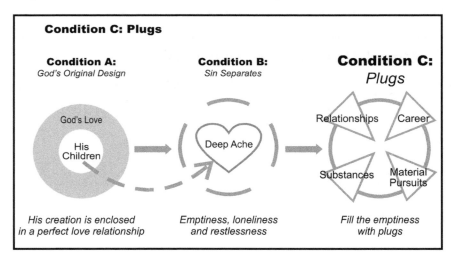

Because Condition B is such a miserable place to exist, we often devote all of our energy toward finding relief. Relief can come from a variety of sources, described as the "plugs" of Condition C. The purpose of a plug is to fill up the holes in Condition B with pleasures, distractions, or pursuits. As a way of avoiding the real issue, our separation from God's love, we pursue plugs to take our mind off the inner emptiness and fill the emptiness with a temporary fix. The solution is only temporary because external solutions will never satisfy our inner needs. Solomon expressed this when he said, God "set eternity in the human heart; yet no one can fathom what God has done from beginning to end" (Eccl. 3:11). With eternity set in our hearts, only that which has eternal significance—namely, what is done under God's power, with his blessing, and for his glory—will provide lasting fulfillment.

Plugs may not be bad things in and of themselves. Their merit is determined by one's purpose for using them. As Mike and I explored the concept of plugs, he suddenly understood why he spent so much time and energy in the pursuit of female companionship, his "plug of choice." The high he experienced at the start of a new relationship was an effective temporary solution for the deep ache in his heart. All too soon, however, the realities of what was required for a deep and lasting relationship kicked in. As the infatuation faded, Mike began searching for the high of a new relationship. Mike's desire for companionship was not a bad thing. Mike desired companionship because that is how God wired us. Now, however, he realized that by operating outside of God's plan for relationships, he was simply using women to fill an emptiness that could only be met by his Creator.

Mike expected his potential partners to accomplish what is humanly impossible, and therefore, set his relationships up for guaranteed failure. Others choose equally ineffective plugs, such as when individuals who are so desperate for relief from loneliness allow themselves to be physically or emotionally abused. They know what is happening is wrong, but choose not to break free from the destructive relationship. If they could put words to their inner pain, they might tell us that "a bad plug is better than no plug."

Others choose plugs like their career, material pursuits, or substances with similar results. When the effects of using a small amount of the plug are not strong enough to numb the pain, more commitment to or preoccupation with the plug is necessary. A plug dependency can quickly develop. For many people the deep ache is so strong they need a combination of plugs. In his state of spiritual and emotional bankruptcy, Mike said the career plug was not working, the substance plug was effective for a while but no longer, and he did not want to hurt any other women by using them as relationship plugs. He laughed and said, "I have never made enough money to get caught up in the material possessions plug."

Some plugs are surprising because they seem so wholesome. Is it possible that children can become a plug? There is nothing wrong with wanting to be the best parent possible, but what if that desire is driven by a need to be needed or to find one's identity in the success or well-being of the children?

Religious involvement provides one of the best plugs available. What could be better than getting praised for doing good deeds while at the same time avoiding one's inner work? Religious involvement as a plug is so effective because it causes us to feel good about ourselves, often provides positive feedback from those we serve, and most importantly leaves us so exhausted that there is no time or energy to "Be still, and know that [he is] God" (Ps. 46:10).

Remember, these items are not bad in and of themselves. Our misuse of them is what makes them a plug. A plug might be physical fitness, shopping, recreation, entertainment, social media, sports, or food. During the past six months four different couples have come to me for counseling because one of the partners was spending excessive time playing online games. In two of the cases, the gaming spouse had developed a strong emotional bond with an opposite gender playing companion. The virtual world provided a captivating way of plugging the painful reminders of a faltering marriage.

Whether due to religious involvements, career demands, trying to give our kids the best, or any of the other demands for our time, many people can relate to Mike's words: "It seems like something is missing." Even as we complain about the pace of life, maybe we resist making changes because the anesthesia of busyness is serving a greater purpose, helping us avoid feeling and facing Condition B. How tragic to realize that one has spent an entire life pursuing a temporarily effective plug, while avoiding the most important life questions. Just as painfully tragic is the realization that much of what goes on in the helping professions is nothing more than finding better ways to manage existing plugs or exploring strategies for incorporating new ones.

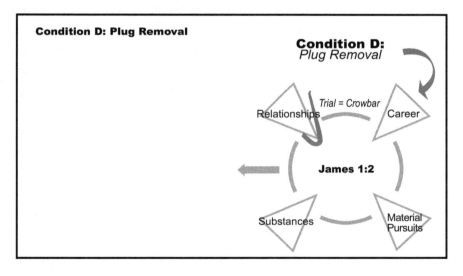

Mike pursued therapy because his plugs were no longer working. I cannot explain why God chooses to come after us when he does, but in Mike's case the process of plug removal had begun. God shows himself as a jealous lover of his people in the book of Hosea (see Hos. 13:4). When he formed a covenant relationship with his chosen people, God made it clear that he would not tolerate their pursuit and worship of other gods (see Ex. 20:3-5). God desired an intimate, exclusive relationship with his people. He desires the same of his people today. As Mike's plugs began to fail, God was in the process of restoring with Mike what a sin-controlled nature had rejected and avoided: an intimate relationship. For this to happen, Mike's plugs had to be removed.

I had a difficult time understanding, let alone applying, the words of the apostle James: "Consider it pure joy, my brothers and sisters, whenever you face trials of many kinds …" (James 1:2) until I saw it as a good description of plug removal. Trials have a way of getting our attention, especially those trials beyond our ability to fix. James was writing to early believers whose well-being was threatened by religious persecution. As their spiritual leader, James wanted the early Christians to know that their trials were serving the purpose of producing something positive in them.

The same principle applies in our growth, as trials become the crowbar God uses to pry out our plugs. Mike realized that his relationship trials were God's crowbar to help him see that this plug was not working and needed to be removed. Plug removal is painful! Letting go of our comfort fixes is never easy. That is why we need help doing it. Why, then, does James describe it as "pure joy"? Finding joy in pain sounds masochistic. In this process, however, the joy comes from knowing that a loving God is pursuing us with the good intentions of restoring us to his original plan, enveloping us in a perfect love relationship. We no longer have to make do with unfulfilling substitutes.

At this point in the process, many people find that their unresolved feelings about God's love begin to surface. Some individuals will describe a time when their sin separated them from God and they cried out to him only to hear no response. Others will remember a time when they were between plugs and they considered God as a possible answer only to find that the churches they visited or the people they knew who claimed to be followers of God seemed uninterested or too distracted by their own problems. Some, like Mike, will admit that they still struggle with the image of a constantly disappointed God. Mike added that, even though as an adult he could accept the idea of a loving God, he did not know if he could expect to ever experience or feel that love. To sort out these issues requires some deep work.

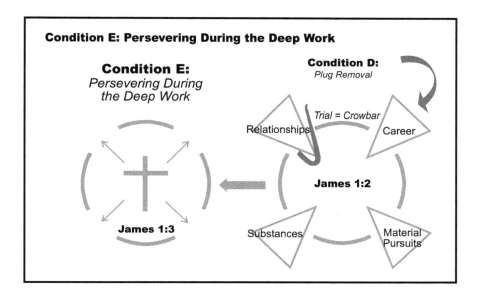

When someone reaches this stage of the process, they realize that their plugs are no longer the solution to what is wrong with their life. God has graciously pried out the ineffective plugs. Now instead of looking for external plugs to make life work better, a change begins to take place from within. Paul used the words "being transformed into [Christ's] image" to describe a process undertaken by every true follower of Jesus (2 Cor. 3:18).

While every believer experiences this process, the speed and degree of change will vary greatly from person to person. In Mike's case, his relational growth was stunted by a history of superficial relationships and therefore moved slowly. On the other hand, he suddenly developed a voracious appetite for God's Word. Mike said, "The Bible lessons and stories I grew up with are now becoming personal. How could something written so long ago be so real today?"

The symbol of the cross with arrows pointing outward in Condition E illustrates that God's rule and his kingdom ways of operating are now permeating all of the person's life. Remember the announcement Jesus made at the beginning of his earthly ministry: "The time has come.... The kingdom of God has come near. Repent and believe the good news!" (Mark 1:15). Whether into the chaotic middle-eastern world of his day, or into the life of a confused twenty-six-year-old named Mike, Jesus' entrance becomes the pivotal point through which everything else is given meaning. With God taking hold of Mike's heart, there was much more honesty in his description of his inner struggles. Honesty led to heartfelt confession, which produced a genuine repentance. Mike described this repentance as "losing my desire for what didn't work." For the first time in his life he believed the good news of what Jesus did to set him free. Mike realized that he had been sitting in a prison cell, when Jesus had already unlocked the door.

Sitting with people as they overcome the despair of being separated from God by their sin, the false hope of plugs, and the painful process of plug extraction takes a toll, but the sheer joy of joining the Spirit in the deep work that is the final stage of this process makes it all worthwhile! I sense Paul was experiencing the exhilaration of watching the Ephesians move into a place of persevering in the deep work when he wrote:

> I pray that out of his glorious riches he may strengthen you with power through his Spirit in your inner being, so that Christ may dwell in your hearts through faith. And I pray that you, being rooted and established in love, may have power, together with all the Lord's holy people, to grasp how wide and long and high and deep is the love of Christ, and to know this love that surpasses knowledge—that you may be filled to the measure of all the fullness of God.
>
> (Eph. 3:16-19)

The transformation process is moving along quite nicely, but we are not out of the woods yet. Perseverance is needed as this new faith gets tested (see James 1:3). Perseverance reminds us that although the plugs are out, they are still lurking. Since transformation is the process of becoming aware, letting go, and being filled with the Holy Spirit, we will continue to experience times when the newness of what is happening is challenged by a longing for what is familiar. Even though Mike knew his plugs were not the answer, he found the old patterns were hard to break. Torn between the new and the comfortably familiar, Mike could relate to Paul's words, "I do not understand what I do. For what I want to do I do not do, but what I hate I do.... For I have the desire to do what is good, but I cannot carry it out" (Rom. 7:15, 18b).

Perseverance means trusting the life-changing process even when it feels like it is not working or is taking too long. During these times of soul searching and uncertainty, the most therapeutic thing a helper can do is offer encouragement for the progress already made, perspective that the current struggle has purpose, and assurance that someone who cares is present. In other words, the helper provides the gift of hope and the fellowship of a true restoration companion.

I was privileged to be Mike's restoration companion as he experienced the transformational change of becoming more like Christ. As he persevered through the highs and lows, the stops and starts of Conditions B through E, he began to get a glimpse of what was available in Condition F. What he saw appeared to be the promised land of completeness in Christ, or as James described it, "let perseverance finish its work so that you may be mature and complete, not lacking anything" (James 1:4).

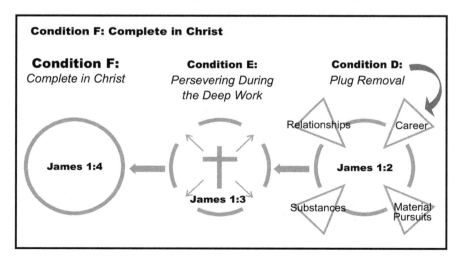

Condition F: Complete in Christ

Condition F:
Complete in Christ

Condition E:
*Persevering During
the Deep Work*

Condition D:
Plug Removal

James 1:4

James 1:3

James 1:2

Relationships

Career

Substances

Material
Pursuits

Our goal is to help people live as close to Condition F as possible. We desire to see them operate from a place of completeness in Christ because that is where they reconnect with God's original plan: a perfect love relationship with creation, each other, and their Creator. Moving toward completeness in Christ allows people to engage in relationships out of the overflow of having been loved well. It is a place of fullness, not longing.

The lies of the plugs are exposed as promises that can't be delivered. A radically transformed heart finds its deepest fulfillment in the oneness that comes from Father, Son, and Spirit intimacy. Chapter 2 provides a deeper look into how to receive God's love as the starting point for everything else we do.

Reflection Questions

1. Which condition (B–E) describes where you live? (You may be in more than one.)

2. What words would you use to describe your Condition B? For example, empty, restless, searching, lonely, discouraged, etc.

3. What are your past and present plugs? Which were / are the hardest to give up?

4. Review your pace of life. To what degree are you at risk for living under the anesthesia of busyness?

5. If you slowed down your pace, what unresolved habits or relationship issues might catch up?

6. Describe your experience of having a plug removed. How did God reveal to you that a particular activity, person, or object was a plug? Were there trials involved?

7. Describe in your words what takes place in the transformational process of Condition E. How much of that have you experienced?

Chapter 2

THE STARTING POINT FOR ALL RELATIONSHIPS

Can you think of any one thing in your life that has generated more pleasure and pain than relationships? We devote considerable time, emotional energy, and money to relationships. It's no wonder we suffer when they are not doing well.

Jesus focused much of his time on building, teaching about, and enjoying relationships. When a religious leader asked him, "Which is the greatest commandment in the Law?" Jesus replied, "Love the Lord your God with all your heart and with all your soul and with all your mind. This is the first and greatest commandment. And the second is like it: Love your neighbor as yourself" (Matt. 22:36-39). In essence, Jesus was saying that there is nothing more important than being in a loving relationship with God and others.

Relationships were the final topic Jesus talked about with his disciples before he ascended to heaven. He told his disciples to go and build relationships with people from all nations so that they, too, could become followers of Christ. At the same time, Jesus told his disciples that he would always be with them (see Matt. 28:16-20). Simply stated, Jesus commissioned his followers to go build life-changing relationships with others, with the full assurance of his life-changing presence in their lives. Throughout the history of the Christian church, one of the greatest hindrances to fulfilling this final command has been the disunity created when Christ-followers cannot get along with each other or are reluctant to accept and build relationships with those who are not like them. The only way to understand God's design and to become an active participant in it is through relationships.

Four Stations

After logging many thousands of hours listening to people struggle with personal problems, I have concluded that there are four primary areas, or "stations," where people need relational help (See diagram on page 33).

Station 1 focuses on our relationship with God as he pours his love and truth into us. One of the major relational challenges in Station 1 is learning how to receive these gifts from God. As we do, they become the foundation for everything that follows.

Station 2 is where we find our only true identity in Christ. "I" work in Station 2 often involves a mixture of relational healing, surrender, and obedience as God's love and truths take hold. One of the significant challenges of working with individuals in Station 2 is helping them to trust the Spirit-guided transformational process that is changing them from the inside out.

Station 3 occurs when two individuals join in a relationship and form a "We." This relationship provides the setting where God's love is passed on to another. It also provides a workshop-like environment where God teaches some of his most important lessons. Often those lessons involve learning how to love and work with individuals who, in our opinion, are at times not very lovable. Learning to develop a humble and teachable spirit is a great way to succeed in Station 3.

Station 4 is where all the previous growth can be used, in gratitude, to benefit others who need to hear and see the good news of God's love. People who reach Station 4 find their kingdom purpose that gives life its true meaning. For helpers, seeing a person they have helped reaching out to others with compassion is a tremendous encouragement.

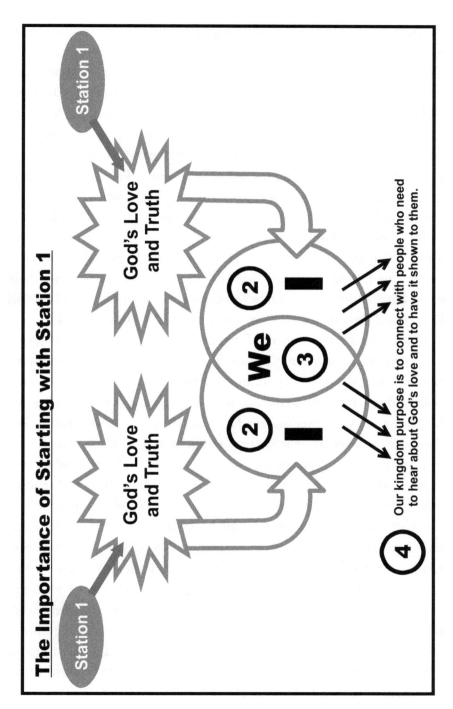

The Importance of Starting with Station 1

Station 1

God's Love and Truth

God's Love and Truth

We

4 Our kingdom purpose is to connect with people who need to hear about God's love and to have it shown to them.

As individuals get rid of their plugs and move toward completeness in Christ, they are preparing themselves for a healthy connection with God and others. Much of what gets talked about in counseling sessions or read about in self-help publications focuses on fixing one's self image and immediate relationships, Stations 2 and 3. This is natural. We want to figure out why we do the things we do (Station 2), and because we are created with a drive for connection we want good relationships with those closest to us (Station 3). Obviously "I" and "We" growth are very important, but as you can see from the diagram, it would be a costly mistake to neglect the other two Stations. Without a strong foundational relationship with God (Station 1), we are limited in how much we can know about ourselves (Station 2), or understand about how to best connect with others (Station 3). At the same time, when we neglect to move beyond our closest relationships to share with others the joy we have found (Station 4), we miss out on life's greatest purpose.

Justin was a self-professed information technology freak. He enjoyed every part of his job, especially his role as network troubleshooter. Justin was known as the go-to guy for difficult problems. His problem-solving skills worked beautifully on the job, but not so well in his marriage. His wife Megan was on stress overload as a first year elementary school teacher. By the end of the school day she was emotionally and physically drained. Justin was quick to diagnose her problem as a time management issue and wasted no time offering suggestions. His intentions were good, but the diagnosis missed the mark and Megan felt talked down to instead of understood.

With his attempts to help rejected, Justin did what most guys do when their advice is not received: He retreated to his world of plugs to fill the relational vacuum. Megan was shocked by the intensity of the resentment she felt toward Justin for pulling away when she desperately needed him.

Justin and Megan were experiencing a total "miss." He was convinced that she was too stubborn to receive his help. She felt that he didn't understand how overwhelmed she was and only wanted to fix things to avoid any further inconvenience to himself. As with most "misses," there was enough truth in both positions to build a justifiable case.

By the time they came in for counseling, their only communication was about the basic essentials of managing a house together. Any other discussions quickly deteriorated into an argument fueled by the festering resentments of a malnourished "We." Neither wanted their marriage to end, but both wondered if they would make it to their sixth anniversary. Megan and Justin, like many couples, were making the mistake of evaluating the future of their relationship based on the current condition of their "We."

Justin and Megan were desperate to receive help with their "We." It definitely needed some restorative work, but there was other work that needed to happen first. I invited them to accept that their "We" needed to be put in the critical care unit and given time to heal. Justin had a hard time believing that the best way to help the "We" was to avoid working on it. Understandably, he expected counseling to be the place where they would learn how to resolve their relationship problems and recapture the excitement of their early years. I assured him that the best way to begin helping their relationship was to spend some time looking at their individual relationships with God and their own personal growth, Stations 1 and 2.

The rationale for this approach is found in Jesus' question, "Why do you look at the speck of sawdust in your brother's eye and pay no attention to the plank in your own eye? ... You hypocrite, first take the plank out of your own eye, and then you will see clearly to remove the speck from your brother's eye" (Matthew 7:3, 5). Jesus makes it clear that the starting point for dealing with relational problems is a personal examination. A Spirit-guided examination leads to appropriate owner-ship of the relational problems, preventing one person from taking too much or too little responsibility. I interpret the spirit of what Jesus taught this way: Before you address what is bothersome about your partner's behavior, the speck, examine the condition of your heart, which is, by way of comparison, a plank.

After a prolonged period of tension, taking some time for personal reflection (Station 2) and spiritual renewal (Station 1) is essential. As a helper, if you encounter resistance to your suggestion for a truce, be prepared: any potentially positive work going forward may be sabotaged by blame, lingering resentment, and defensiveness. When couples have trouble breaking out of hurtful patterns of communicating, it can be useful to let them see how destructive these patterns are. I will sometimes allow them to start heating up, only to interrupt them and ask, "Is what you are doing right now helpful?" "Was it helpful the last time you two spoke to each other this way?" "Has it ever been helpful?" "Then why continue doing something that has never worked, and in fact, has made things much worse?" Once they see that their "We" is fragile and likely only to be damaged by premature attempts to fix it, many are willing to take a step back and regroup in Stations 1 and 2.

 Pause to Consider

It is not uncommon to see work-related strengths become liabilities at home. Justin's strength was his ability to analyze a situation, determine what was not working properly, and then take decisive action to fix it. This approach works well on the job because it is efficient and gets results. This approach is not so effective at home because, believe it or not, spouses do not like to be seen as a problem to be fixed.

As I began to show Justin the error of his impersonal approach, to my dismay I realized I was doing to him what he had been doing to Megan. I was implementing a "fix it" approach to "fix" his "fix it" approach.

One of the hardest habits to break in beginning counselors, lay or professional, is the irresistible urge to be a "fixer."

After we laughed at the hypocrisy of my approach, I made a mid-course correction. I went back and affirmed Justin for what he had done well. His attempt to diagnose and fix were interpreted as his way of showing concern. We even determined that his conclusions were correct. What was missing was a meaningful, relational connection with Megan throughout the process. She added a hearty YES to this observation.

I had the opportunity to model how to reconnect as I cleaned up my mistake. Yes, humility is required. We moved forward in our discussions with a renewed commitment to see things from the other person's perspective. We also agreed to examine the condition of our hearts before giving feedback. From this experience and many others, I am continually reminded that the best way to facilitate change is through relational acceptance and trust.

Station 1: God's Love and Truth

Entering Station 1 requires going to God and saying, "You're the one who created relationships; help me clean up the mess I've made of this one." When we do this, God responds, "Let me show you how relational I am and what tremendous plans I have for you and your spouse or close friendships; but first let's look at *our* relationship." Station 1 is built on the premise that, as we spend time with him, God delights to give us everything we need for healthy connections with others.

Moses provides an excellent example of receiving from God first what he later needed to relate effectively with the people he was chosen to lead, the Israelites. Moses experienced an extended time in Station 1 as he met with God on Mount Sinai (see Ex. 24:12). With his holiness on full display on the mountain, God spoke to Moses in a personal way "as one speaks to a friend" (Ex. 33:11). God took great care to give Moses specific guidelines for how to be in relationship with him and with the people he was called to lead. I find great comfort in watching God give Moses what he needed, even before Moses knew he needed it. Moses was learning how to receive from God first what he would soon need for the specific challenges of leading "a stiff-necked people" (Ex. 32:9).

In addition to ceremonial guidelines and commandments, Moses needed help learning how to manage his frustrations as a leader. In a wonderfully personal way, God revealed his own intense anger toward the people at their violation of the first of his Ten Commandments. Seeing the people worshipping a golden calf they created, God's response was, "Now leave me alone so that my anger may burn against them and that I may destroy them" (Ex. 32:10). What happened next in the account is amazing. Moses pleaded with God, reminding God of his promises to the patriarchs and of his reputation among the other nations. Moses, caught up in the moment, may have actually thought God needed to be reminded of these things. God had a purpose, though, in showing Moses his white-hot anger and then using Moses to help him relent from bringing on the disaster (see Ex. 32:14). All too soon, Moses would encounter the same idolatrous behavior that infuriated God. In response, Moses would throw down the hand-carved tablets and smash them into pieces. Was it a righteous display of anger or a displeasing outburst?

In this Station 1 time of preparation, God modeled anger management for Moses. It was a God-orchestrated dress rehearsal. The violent temper that killed the Egyptian soldier, smashed the tablets, and struck the rock twice, thus preventing Moses from entering the Promised Land, needed attention. On the mountain, in the aftermath of Israel's idolatry, Moses was allowed to see God's anger and to be a part of God's cooling off period to show Moses how it could be done. God was committed to preparing Moses to be the leader he needed to be for Israel. God is just as committed to helping each of us in our much needed areas of relationship preparation, if we are willing to spend the time lingering in his presence long enough to learn how to be loved and prepared.

Consider the implications of what God wants to give us in Station 1. Many marriages end because of the real or perceived deficiencies of a spouse. According to the promise of Station 1, the problem may not be one spouse's deficiencies; instead, it may be the divorcing party's refusal to receive from God what is needed to love their spouse well. Handling a difficult partner requires careful discernment. The goal of spending time in Station 1 is to ensure that decisions are made after sitting quietly in God's presence listening for guidance and then acting with the full assurance that strength will be given for whatever action is needed.

As a helper you may have already experienced how hard it is for some people to slow down, be still in God's presence, and receive what he wants to give them. If you can get them to slow their pace and quiet the internal noise, your second major challenge will be to help them learn how to be loved and carried by God through difficult circumstances.

Megan knew that God loved her. She just didn't know how to be loved by him. Whether she felt loved by God was directly related to how well she carried out her religious practices such as Bible reading, prayer, and church attendance. Spending all day teaching and all night creating lesson plans left her with little time or energy for Justin or God. She had a gnawing sense that maybe the problems in her marriage were God's way of punishing her.

In your role as a helper, perhaps you have already reached the conclusion that it is really hard to help people who have a messed up theology! Several years ago I was in a staff meeting with a group of highly respected Christian clinicians, including several psychiatrists, psychologists, professional counselors, and social workers. Someone asked, "If you could give your clients one thing that would help them get better, what would it be?" After bouncing around several ideas, one of my colleagues suggested, "The one thing I wish for all my clients in their journey toward healing and health is a correct image of who God is." Megan and Justin had carried the image of a disappointed God for so long, that Station 1 had little appeal—so they had simply avoided it.

In my years of counseling, I have consistently observed that problems in Station 3 mirror the problems in Station 1. For example, if it is difficult to receive God's love or to trust his way of taking care of things, it will be difficult to trust or be fully loved by a spouse or close friend. The good news for Justin and Megan, and others like them, is what can happen when honest dialogue with God begins. It may take days, weeks, or even months, but as long as the dialogue continues there is hope for a gradual softening of the heart and a growing awareness of God's pursuit.

Megan's breakthrough came one morning on her way to work. With tears in her eyes, Megan described how, out of nowhere, God spoke to her heart and said, "I really enjoy watching you pour yourself into struggling students. I receive this as an act of worship." This simple thought radically altered how Megan viewed what it meant to spend time with God. Where previously she had seen spending time with God as sitting quietly or reading the Bible, she began to see how God meets us in a wide variety of life experiences. Far from discarding her "quiet time," as Megan's perspective changed she began to actually look forward to being still in God's presence as a way to be prepared for the daily encounters. Megan and Justin soon described Station 1 as the place where the Holy Spirit applied God's Word directly to them and then took what was in their hearts and turned it into prayers and praise before God's throne.

As a helper, be careful to avoid the tendency to try to fix relationship problems before time is spent in Stations 1 and 2. Only in the context of Station 1 will those we help learn that:

- God promises to give us first in our relationship with him what will be required in our relationships with others.
- The starting point for dealing with our relational problems is a personal/spiritual examination.
- Incorrect images of God interfere with the development of healthy relationships.
- The ability to quiet the inner noise and listen to the promptings of the Holy Spirit is essential for our spiritual, personal, and relational development.

Reflection Questions

1. Identify a problem you are experiencing in an important relationship. What might God want to give or teach you in Station 1 to help you with your current challenge?

2. Megan knew that God loved her. She just didn't know how to be loved by him. Give some specific ways God has shown and is showing his love to you. How easy is it for you to receive his love?

3. How does living as one who is loved well by God affect your interactions with others?

4. What are some potentially incorrect images of God you may be carrying? How are they interfering with your desire to be in relationship with him?

5. Where are you at risk for setting up Station 3 relationships to fail by demanding something from them you were invited to receive first from God in Station 1?

6. As you commit to becoming more conscious of living in Station 1, how easy is it for you to quiet the internal noises and churning? Is there someone God has placed in your life that can help you grow in this area?

Chapter 3

TRANSFORMING THE "I" PART

Station 2: The Process of Transformation

With the full assurance that God will provide everything that is needed, we are now ready to begin the transformational work required in the "I" part of Station 2. Based on our own growth and our experiences helping others, we know all too well that the natural tendency of the "I" is to resist any change that prevents it from doing what it wants, when it wants. If we want to see growth happen, we need to find a way to overcome that natural tendency to resist change.

For believers, the ability to change comes when we put our faith in Christ and a unique and powerful change agent is turned loose on our "I": the Holy Spirit. His primary goal is to remove all influences of the old "I" and replace them with his presence. Paul described this exchange when he wrote, "Therefore, if anyone is in Christ, the new creation has come: The old has gone, the new is here!" (2 Cor. 5:17). There is sacredness to this process of Holy Spirit change. In an earlier letter to the Corinthian believers, Paul made it clear that the "I" space is holy. He described it as God's temple, the place where his Spirit resides (see 1 Cor. 6:19).

The diagram above shows the flow of God's love and truth from Station 1 into the "I" circle of Station 2, which we now view as God's temple. Those of us who help others can participate in the Holy Spirit's miraculous work of transforming corrupt natures into Christ-likeness. As we walk with people through the process of receiving God's love and applying his truth, we realize that these words are more than just nice things to talk about—they are life-changing forces!

The changes taking place in a person's life will not go unnoticed, nor should they. A changed life cannot help but draw attention. Some will discount the change, much like the onlookers at Pentecost who attributed the movement of the Holy Spirit through Jesus' disciples to drunkenness (see Acts 2:12, 13). Others will find the change contagious and will want to know more. Part of our job as helpers is not only to help people understand what is happening in their lives, but also to prepare them to share God's love and truth with others. We will talk more about how the overflow of God's love is spread to others when we discuss Stations 3 and 4. For now, let's explore how we can facilitate the life-changing work taking place in Station 2.

As we join individuals in their transformational journey, it is important to acknowledge our common starting point. "For all have sinned and fall short of the glory of God" (Rom. 3:23). According to this verse, helpers and the people they help have something in common: They are both sinners and unless sin is removed, death will create an eternal separation from God. Sin is not just something we do wrong; as members of the human race, it is the condition into which we are born and there is nothing any of us can do to make it right on our own. Acknowledging our corrupt nature allows us to drop the pretense of trying to be someone we are not. As helpers, we humbly recognize that anything we have to offer others is a result of the amazing grace of Jesus applied to our hearts. When we experience what it means to have Christ enter our lives and set us free from the grip of a sinful nature, we are compelled to share this message of hope with others. We have the opportunity to model how to do this with the people we help.

Seeing those we help as sinners may not seem like a very positive way to view them. Ironically though, this viewpoint can be a very refreshing place to start your work together. Ask yourself this important question: Am I more interested in treating the effects of sin or in helping people become free from sin itself? The effects of sin are all around us. When we see what sin has done to attack the bodies, relationships, and overall well-being of those who come to us for help, the desire to help them find relief from the ravages of sin is a natural response and a worthy endeavor. This isn't, however, the model we see when we study how Jesus responded to the needs of people. For example, when Jesus was asked a question, how many times did he answer it directly? The answer, it turns out, is rarely. Instead of getting sidetracked with superficial discussions about customs and practices, the usual focus of the questions he was asked, with laser-like precision Jesus exposed the attitudes and motives of those asking the questions. In his example, we observe a pattern of meeting people where they were, but not being satisfied with letting them stay there.

On one occasion when the Pharisees and teachers of the law questioned Jesus about why his disciples were breaking the tradition of the elders by not washing their hands before eating, he turned the question back on them by asking, "Why do you break the command of God for the sake of your tradition?" (Matt. 15:3) Jesus then went on to challenge the Pharisees on their practice of using a loophole in the law to withhold care to their elderly, dependent parents. While the Pharisees were upset about the disciples not having clean hands, Jesus focused on the impurity of the Pharisees' hearts and how they were hurting others. Quoting the prophet Isaiah, Jesus responded, "These people honor me with their lips, but their hearts are far from me" (Matt. 15:8). In essence Jesus was saying, "You may think this is important, but let me show you what is really at stake. Let me love you by responding to the question you need to be asking." Jesus did not do Band-Aid fixes! His responses laid bare the conditions of peoples' hearts because he knew that was the only place where permanent healing could occur.

As helpers following his model, we also need to meet people where they are and then begin a process of walking with them as the Holy Spirit exposes the deeper issues of the heart, things like desires, motives, rejections, fears, selfishness, and unmet needs to be loved. If left unexposed and unexplored, these forces have a detrimental influence on every part of our lives. But even when they are exposed, change does not come easily. It is tempting to assume that when people see the real issues, they will naturally want to fix them. But then we remember all the times the Holy Spirit has revealed areas of needed change in our own lives and our response was to resist. One of the best predictors of success in your work with people is their degree of receptivity to the Holy Spirit's efforts to take control of these forces.

Jesus drove this principle home in his parable about spreading seeds on different types of soil, highlighting the various degrees of receptivity to hearing and receiving the Word of God as delivered through the Holy Spirit. At the end of the parable Jesus quoted the prophet Isaiah, "For this people's *heart has become calloused*; they hardly hear with their ears, and they have closed their eyes. Otherwise they might see with their eyes, hear with their ears, understand with their hearts and turn, and I would heal them" (Matt. 13:15, emphasis added). How many no's does it take to create a calloused heart? It is impossible to come up with a set number, but it is not hard to appreciate what a dangerous condition this is. How many yes's does it take to open the flood gate of resurrection power that raised Christ from the dead and to experience life as one who is free from the old nature? Just one!

Have you ever considered how many Holy Spirit-prompted moments of decision occur each day: one, two, twenty, fifty …? Perhaps without even realizing it, multiple times each day we are saying either yes or no to the Spirit's offer of help, healing, instruction, or empowerment. It's no wonder many of us muddle through each day in our Christian journey doing the best we can, all the while believing that the really big accomplishments are done by people who have been given amazing revelations and knock-you-off-your-feet encounters with God. Without discounting the fact that God can and does manifest himself in dramatic fashion for some people, I've finally begun to understand that the basic building blocks of spiritual growth often come in the form of everyday "Holy Spirit-prompted moments of decision."

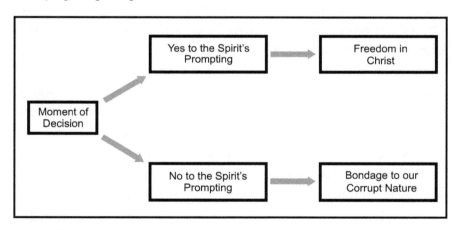

Since much of our work in helping others takes place in the battleground of the mind, it should come as no surprise that many Spirit-prompted moments of decision target our thought patterns. Here are a few examples of moments of decision that can occur in our thought life.

- How far do we allow our minds to wander into impure or unhealthy places before we catch ourselves?
- At what point do we become aware that our "entertainment" is filling our minds with images that degrade who we were designed to be?
- How many really unhealthy beliefs about the way the world should work and others should treat us do we rigidly carry?
- What are the recurring thoughts we have about our inadequacies?

After a moment of silence during a counseling session, I asked Joe what he was thinking. He said his mind was wandering all over the map, so I asked, "What are some of the places your mind is taking you to and are they helpful?"

Joe paused for a moment and said, "We were talking about my short fuse and I flashed back to the harsh words I've had with my thirteen-year-old son. The final straw was his report card which contained two D's for not turning in assignments." I decided to take advantage of a here-and-now opportunity to show Joe how his thought patterns were working against him. Joe's mistake was in giving his thoughts free rein to go wherever they wanted. Because of his racing mind, he just assumed this was normal. It had never occurred to him that he controlled how much time he spent dwelling on a particular thought.

The Apostle Paul had to deal with criticisms, misrepresentations, and outright lies about himself and about God's work. He described his strategy for combating the effects of these falsehoods in his own life in this way: "We demolish arguments and every pretension that sets itself up against the knowledge of God, and we take captive every thought to make it obedient to Christ" (2 Cor. 10:5). Paul was dealing with attacks from outside forces, but I believe his example is useful for the battles we wage for control over our internal thought processes.

Using Paul's example, I pulled Joe out of his unfiltered thought process, modeling for him what the Holy Spirit does when he prompts us in those moments of clarity and decision, helping us to turn our thoughts in another direction. As Joe responded by taking his thoughts captive, he was able to identify the options he had in his moment of decision.

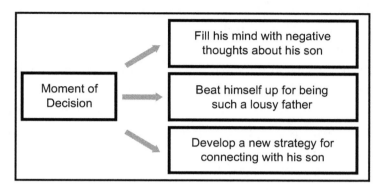

 Pause to Consider

I am a firm believer that "here and now" is always better than "then and there." What do I mean? Joe and I could talk about his thought patterns pertaining to his rocky relationship with his son. We could explore helpful strategies for how to catch and replace negative thinking, how to clean up the guilt from past mistakes, and even how to prevent future ones. As helpful as these conversations would be in addressing what happened or could happen (then and there), talking about what is currently happening (here and now) is much more beneficial because it is experiential learning.

The turning point in our meeting occurred when Joe was triggered by a memory related to his short fuse. As he got lost in the memory of how he interacted with his son, I had a "here and now" moment to work with him on his thought patterns. We were making adjustments to something that was happening in the moment. It allowed me to take full advantage of all the energy and potential that comes with a teachable moment. Joe had a first-hand experience in learning how to capture his thoughts and to choose where he would go with them.

Even when we recognize the moment of decision and desire to respond positively to the Spirit, the ensuing struggle reveals how hard the old nature fights to remain in control. The "I" work of Station 2 is where these battles for control take place.

As we move deeper into the "I" work, we need to be clear that sin was defeated once and for all with Christ's death and resurrection. All we need now is help in learning how to apply the victory! If someone you are helping fears what sin can still do to them, you may want to describe their sin as a paper tiger. It looks ferocious, but at the name of Jesus it disintegrates.

In the book of Revelation, John described a scene in which he wept because no one as worthy to open the scroll. His weeping stopped as he witnessed the Lamb who was slain coming forward to take the scroll. With a crescendo of worship around him, the Lamb was proclaimed worthy because he was slain and with his blood he purchased men and women for God (see Rev. 5)! To be purchased by his blood means we are totally his, totally clean, and totally protected from the grasp of the enemy who would like nothing more than to destroy us. The purchase is complete; nothing more can be added or taken away. We cannot renegotiate the terms of the purchase by falsely believing more good works are needed or that a failure to measure up cancels the purchase. Any future attempts to renegotiate the terms imply that the purchase price of Jesus' blood was insufficient.

In the next chapter we will see how God used Nehemiah as his helper to care for a nation of distraught people. The comparisons between how he restored a nation and how he transforms individuals may be surprising.

Reflection Questions:

1. What is the difference between treating the effects of sin and helping someone move toward freedom from sin?

2. What are some other examples in the gospels of Jesus meeting people where they were, but not being satisfied with letting them stay there?

3. How in tune and receptive are you to the promptings of the Holy Spirit in your role as a helper? See if you can recall some specific examples.

4. Several examples of Spirit-prompted moments of decision in our thought patterns were given. What are some other areas where the Spirit is actively involved in those moments of decision?

5. What are some thoughts that you need to take captive?

6. Where are you at risk for trying to renegotiate the terms of the purchase?

Chapter 4

NEHEMIAH'S MODEL FOR HELPING OTHERS

Station 2 Continued

As we continue to work on the "I" part of our relationships, we should now be able to see some distinct progress. The degree of change corresponds to the decisions made in three primary areas.

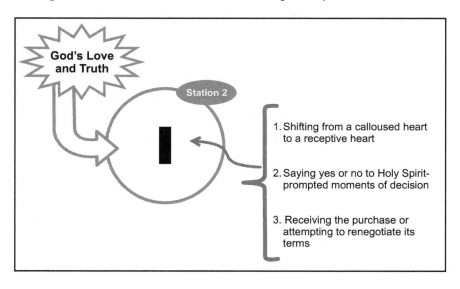

Progress in any of these three areas gets us closer to the goal of removing a self-focused "I" from the control seat of our own lives or the life of the person we are helping. As more and more of the contaminants from the old, sin nature fade away from the "I" part, we begin to see the beauty that was there all along, hidden by all the grime and sludge of sin and self. We begin to see the "I" part as God sees it. What God sees is pleasing to him because it is his "handiwork, created in Christ Jesus to do good works, which God prepared in advance for us to do" (Eph. 2:10).

To view oneself as pleasing to God requires a significant shift in perspective for some people. The shift becomes easier when we realize that God can be pleased with the workmanship of our lives because he sees what we are becoming, even though there is still much more work to be done. In our human perspective, we often miss the beauty of the workmanship because we focus on what is yet to be done and assume that God must be equally disappointed and impatient with our progress. We need to replace the image of a disappointed, impatient God with that of a compassionate God who takes great pleasure in the process.

In Exodus 19 God gives Moses a message for the nation of Israel that I believe is relevant for every believer. God instructs Moses to speak these words to the Israelites: "You yourselves have seen what I did in Egypt, and how I ... brought you to myself.... Now if you obey me fully and keep my covenant, then out of all the nations you will be my treasured possession" (Ex. 19:4, 5). In essence God is saying, "I delight in carefully guiding you away from your place of slavery to your new identity as my *treasured possession.*"

To fully understand the degree of God's involvement in shaping his people and to appreciate what he brings of himself to the process, we need only compare how he guides the formation of our "I" to how he prepared the Israelites to be in relationship with him. The Old Testament book of Nehemiah provides a helpful example. In an inspiring speech, Nehemiah masterfully connected the Israelites' return from Babylonian captivity with the exodus from their slavery in Egypt (see Neh. 9). In both those journeys, when the people faced a critical juncture in their development as a nation, God responded to their cries for help and began a very calculated process of shaping them through a series of difficult transitions. In Nehemiah's time as in Moses's, the people would learn how to get along with each other, trust their leader, and rely on God for everything from their basic needs to victory over powerful adversaries. At each turn, the people were invited to get to know some attribute of God as he revealed himself in very personal ways.

Nehemiah was led by God to begin the process of restoring the nation after their Babylonian captivity. Due to their persistent hardness of hearts, and after many prophetic warnings, God had brought judgment on the people and had allowed them to be conquered and sent into exile. Much like the removal of plugs from an individual, God needed to remove the plugs of idolatry from the nation of Israel. Once their worship of idols was removed, Nehemiah returned to rebuild the walls of Jerusalem and renew the faith of the people. Nehemiah, in his role as a helper, became God's instrument for restoration. One of the primary ways Nehemiah facilitated transformation was revealing the different facets of God that the people needed at critical points in their journey.

God's Supremacy

During a day set aside for reading the Law, confessing sins, and praising God, Nehemiah provided the people with an overview of God's past involvement in their development as a nation and his promise for what lay ahead. He started with a clear description of God's pre-eminence. "Blessed be your glorious name, and may it be exalted above all blessing and praise. You alone are the LORD" (Neh. 9:5b, 6a). Once we have a proper perspective of who God is, we understand clearly why we must relinquish the control seat of our lives. With a new awareness of God's power, holiness, and love for us, why would we even want to have control? We can learn from our co-helpers in the addictions arena: The first step toward recovery is the recognition of who has the power to change things and who does not. Only God can provide the kind of deep change of the heart that we are seeking.

God as Creator and Life-Giver

Nehemiah continued by describing God as the Creator and Life-giver. For a nation that had lived for over one hundred years amid the rubble of a destroyed city, the image of God as Creator and Life-giver was a desperately needed vision.

Like them, we as individuals can live for years in the rubble of unexplored or unfinished work in our lives. There is no greater joy than to watch God's Spirit replace someone's inner deadness with his life-giving presence. This kind of change is not easy, but individuals experiencing the unsettledness of having their "I" parts radically changed can be helped by the reassurance that the Creator who set all of life into motion knows how to guide them through this process.

God as Covenant-Maker and Keeper

Nehemiah next proceeded to describe God as Covenant-maker and keeper. This theme runs throughout Scripture. Abraham was the starting point for the old covenant, God's promise to create and call to himself a people from the descendants of Abraham. Centuries later, Jesus ushered in a new covenant to call people from every nation, tribe, and tongue to be God's people.

God's covenant promises remain intact. Today, however, instead of the land and descendants promised to Abraham, God promises us a new home with him in heaven and he promises to do whatever is necessary in our "I" part to prepare us to enjoy our eternal fellowship with him. As Covenant-initiator and keeper, God is saying, "I desire a relationship with you, and not just any relationship. I want a relationship that is exclusive, where I am the deepest desire of your heart and you of mine."

In a day of broken promises between husbands and wives, employers and employees, and politicians and their constituents, the concept of a covenant relationship is often viewed with cynicism. We do not need to be cynical about God's covenant promise, however. We can take hope from Paul's words written while in chains: "being confident of this, that he who began a good work in you will carry it on to completion until the day of Christ Jesus" (Phil. 1:6).

God as Deliverer

In his litany of God's attributes, Nehemiah continued with words that had great historical significance for the Israelites. He reminded the people that their God was a Deliverer (see Neh. 9:9-12). They knew well the stories of how God sent miraculous signs and wonders against Pharaoh, divided the sea for their escape, and provided nature's version of a GPS by using pillars of clouds and fire.

These words continue to have tremendous personal significance for us today. Our God is still in the business of delivering people from trouble. As you help those who are struggling, invite them to name their areas of emotional, mental, or relational captivity, and to meditate on the image of God as Deliverer. If they have trouble identifying these places, you can guide their search by asking about the times or situations when they feel pain or sadness. As they identify their personal places of captivity, you can then point them to the Deliverer who takes us from the bondage of sin to freedom in Christ, from emotional wounds to healing, from fear and anxiety to peace, and from the lies that paralyze to the truth that sets us free.

God's Words

In both Moses's and Nehemiah's day, freedom from captivity brought the opportunity to develop a national identity. In order for the Israelites to function as the people of God, they needed guidelines for how to relate to him and to one another. God provided these guidelines through the instructions he gave to Moses at Mount Sinai. God's guidelines were transmitted through regulations, laws, decrees, and commandments (see Neh. 9:13, 14). One thousand years later, Nehemiah knew that if the people once again heard the words of God, their hearts would be stirred. He also knew that the only way to ensure that their new commitment to God would be sustained was to have it firmly grounded on these same truths.

Our transformation is no different. Helpers who know how to properly handle God's Word will allow it to do what only it can do. "For the word of God is alive and active. Sharper than any double-edged sword, it penetrates even to dividing soul and spirit, joints and marrow; it judges the thoughts and attitudes of the heart" (Heb. 4:12). In order to battle the heresies from outsiders and disunity from insiders, Paul admonished the Colossians to "Let the message of Christ dwell among you richly as you teach and admonish one another with all wisdom ..." (Col. 3:16). The Word of God—applied to the "I" condition, presented in the context of a loving relationship, and under the full influence of the Holy Spirit—produces permanent change!

God's Character

Nehemiah next reminded his listeners of a dark period in their nation's history. He described a time when the people were arrogant, stiff-necked, and disobedient to the commands of God (see Neh. 9:16). Because of these attitudes, the nation went through a prolonged period of repeated rebellion followed by merciful restoration. The reason the people were not totally consumed by their enemies is found in Nehemiah's description of God's character. "But you are a forgiving God, gracious and compassionate, slow to anger and abounding in love. Therefore you did not desert them ..." (Neh. 9:17b).

As the people you are helping experience setbacks, willfully turn away from God, or become discouraged with their progress, be sure your responses reflect God's character. He knows that his helpers, as well as those being helped, are going to mess up. As we experience his love so freely given in response to our mistakes, we are motivated to honor that love by not presumptuously taking advantage of it.

God's Patience

With the Israelites, as with some of us, it was possible to be so arrogant, stiff-necked, and persistently disobedient that for their own protection, God intervened. With the nation of Israel, being conquered by a foreign power was the crisis that finally prompted them to turn their hearts back to God. It takes considerable discernment, though, to know the difference between when God is intervening by creating difficult circumstances in order to get a person's attention and when God is simply allowing that person to experience the consequences of their choices.

I received a call this week from Henry. Henry and I last met two years ago. Our previous meetings focused on helping him heal from an abusive relationship in his past and addressing marital difficulties in his present. Our work in healing from the past traumas went well; the marital work not so well. After two years of unsuccessfully trying to repair his marriage, Henry's stubbornness yielded to his better judgment and he called for help. I'm glad he called before the relationship was lost. Henry is a good reminder that growth often comes in installments. Even when your work together seems to end prematurely, don't give up hope, because a stiff neck can get painfully sore.

 Pause to Consider

What is the difference between being patient with people and enabling unhealthy behavior? I don't always get this right, but I try to be patient with individuals like Henry who are willing to work at making things better, even if their efforts are misguided.

I am less patient with individuals like Carl who only call when there is a crisis. When the consequences for bad choices kick in, Carl is very motivated to get to the root of his problems. As soon as everything settles down and he gets some relief, Carl reverts to his familiar patterns

---

and drops out of counseling. After the third crisis cycle, it became apparent that I was enabling Carl's avoidance pattern and that he was not benefitting from our work. It was time to define our counseling relationship. Carl and I discussed his situation and concluded that this pattern was not helping him. His options were to commit to doing the deeper work with me or to work with another counselor who might be a better match.

I believe God is mercifully patient with our efforts, even our failures, just as he was with the Israelites. I also believe he lovingly confronts a willful disobedience or avoidance so that true restoration is possible, just as he did with the Israelites. May God give you the discernment and grace to know the difference between being patient with people who are trying and enabling the unhealthy patterns of people who are avoiding.

God's Encouragement

Discouragement is a formidable foe in the restoration process. Nehemiah faced it constantly. The prized city, Jerusalem, was in shambles, the strenuous working conditions were made even more difficult by threats of attack by the enemy, and to add insult to injury, some of the leaders were placing extreme financial hardship on the workers (see Neh. 4, 5). Nehemiah did not minimize the discouragement. He had gone through his own time of mourning when he first heard the news about the condition of Jerusalem. "The wall of Jerusalem is broken down, and its gates have been burned with fire. When I heard these things, I sat down and wept. For some days I mourned and fasted and prayed before the God of heaven" (Neh. 1:3b, 4). His empathy for what the people were going through earned him even more of their respect as someone who could be trusted.

Helpers who have gone through painful seasons of discouragement in their lives are uniquely qualified to walk with others. The term "wounded healers" is used to describe individuals who use their own difficult experiences as catalysts for personal growth and are then able to extend the healing they have received to others. Paul's words describe it well. "Praise be to the God and Father of our Lord Jesus Christ, the Father of compassion and the God of all comfort, who comforts us in all our troubles, so that we can comfort those in any trouble with the comfort we ourselves receive from God" (2 Cor. 1:3-4).

God's Faithfulness

Another way Nehemiah confronted a spirit of discouragement was to remind the people of all the ways God provided for them in the past. David's prayers and songs in the Psalms reflect a similar strategy of drawing from God's faithfulness in the past to combat periods of great discouragement. Nehemiah drew from the example of God's provision throughout the journey from Egypt to the Promised Land. He rallied the people with reminders of how God had provided pillars of clouds and fire for guidance, manna for food, water for their thirst, clothing that did not wear out during a forty-year desert pilgrimage (see Neh. 9:19-21), and the inheritance of a fertile land that provided so richly for the people that "they reveled in your great goodness" (Neh. 9:25).

When appropriate, you may want to consider having the people you are helping make a timeline of the difficult periods in their lives. What led up to those times and how did they manage the difficulty? For some, this will be an opportunity to review God's provisions in the past. Even though God may be working differently today, they may be able to glean general principles from how God worked in their lives in the past.

For others, their timeline may be a painful reminder of their disappointment with God's apparent lack of intervention. This presents an opportunity to explore their negative images of God and where they are stuck in their relationship with him. Don't shy away from this discussion. The freedom to be honest about their frustration may be just what is needed for them to re-engage in a dialogue about and eventually with God.

God's Provisions

Nehemiah's description of the Promised Land bounty must have made the people's hearts long for God to restore them to their former prosperity. Remembering everything he had done in their past likely stirred in their hearts a desire to see him do even greater things in their future.

One of the ways to measure progress in the "I" work is through a similar review of God's provisions. I measure true "I" growth when individuals begin to see their "Promised Land" not as an opportunity for personal gain, but as a place where they can be used by God to make a difference in the lives of others. In other words, God's provisions should create in us an excitement and anticipation for how we can be used by him to advance his kingdom. Turning my focus away from what is wrong with me to how I can help others indicates a significant shift toward Christ-likeness.

In the next chapter we will confront the place where the old "I" makes its last stand in an attempt to slow down the transformational momentum that is building. It is time to expose the lies that have held us captive for far too long.

Reflection Questions:

1. Nehemiah started his restorative work by having the people set aside a day to focus on who God is and the way he works. If you are not doing so already, how could you incorporate a similar practice in your life and in the lives of those you are helping?

2. In a spirit of worship Nehemiah told the story of Israel's growth as a nation. He was careful to highlight specific facets of God that stood out during critical times in their development. How could Nehemiah's model be applied in your role as a helper?

3. Which facets of God's nature are the easiest / hardest for you to embrace?

Chapter 5

THE INNER ROOM ℰ

Station 2 Continued

With all the focus on the "I," it might be easy to think that this work is about self-improvement. The attention given the "I" is not to elevate it or, worse, glorify it. The goal of this work is to experience the true freedom that comes from finding one's real identity in Christ and then seeing how that new awareness of true identity will be used to benefit others.

In order to establish a new identity in Christ, something must happen to our old way of looking at ourselves and all it represented. The degree to which an individual is willing to go from old to new determines the depth and sustainability of the change. Jesus left no room for misinterpretation when he told his followers, "…Whoever wants to be my disciple must deny themselves and take up their cross and follow me. For whoever wants to save their life will lose it, but whoever loses their life for me will find it. What good will it be for someone to gain the whole world, yet forfeit their soul?" (Matt. 16:24-26a). We can only get an exchanged identity by crucifying the old. Paul told the Galatians, "I have been crucified with Christ and I no longer live, but Christ lives in me" (Gal. 2:20).

As a helper guiding people through this process of change, do not be surprised if many of the people who come to you for help are caught between holding on and letting go. They may like the idea of Jesus living in them, while not feeling quite as comfortable with the concept of "I no longer live." In some ways these people are the easiest to work with because of their honesty. You might find it helpful to remind them that Jesus also went through a lengthy process of preparing for his crucifixion, starting with the very beginning of his adult journey as recorded in Scripture.

As Jesus launched his public ministry we get a glimpse into his Station 2 "I" space. Jesus asked John to baptize him. John recognized how inappropriate it was for a sinful man to baptize the sinless Son of Man, but Jesus persisted and John relented. In this act of humility, Jesus symbolically revealed himself as the one who would conquer sin. During his baptism, two significant events took place. "At that moment heaven was opened, and he saw the Spirit of God descending like a dove and alighting on him. And a voice from heaven said, 'This is my Son, whom I love; with him I am well pleased'" (Matt. 3:16-17). In this amazing event we see Jesus' "I" part filled with humility, the full anointing of the Spirit, and God's pronouncement of love and approval. What a great way to launch a ministry! Why then did the Spirit of God lead Jesus into the wilderness for forty days of fasting and exposure to the devil's temptations? Anything we could possibly hope to gain from such a time of fasting, Jesus already had.

The answer to the question is found in the three temptations. Jesus' wilderness fasting and temptation addressed the issues of provision, care, and success. In the first recorded temptation Jesus was ending his fast and would naturally need some sustenance to move forward. Satan urged Jesus, *Why not use your spiritual resources to provide for your needs? Turn the stones into bread and you'll be good to go* (see Matt. 4:1). Nowhere in the gospels do we find an example of Jesus using his spiritual resources for his personal comfort. Instead, starting with this first temptation, Jesus allowed God to provide in his own way and in his own timing.

In his second temptation, Satan reminded Jesus that he would soon be entering into some difficult situations. Could he trust that God would care for him properly? *Why not test it out right now by jumping off the pinnacle of the temple and seeing if the angels are able to care for you?* (see Matt: 4:6). This temptation subtly went beyond questioning God's ability to care for Jesus' needs. Satan encouraged Jesus to control how God's care should be given. (As people wrestle through their life crises, their struggle is typically not with God's ability, but with his failure to respond the way they think he should.)

Satan concluded his temptations by attempting to place a seed of doubt in Jesus' mind about whether he would be successful. *Young man starting out in ministry, how do you know how your message will be received? For a price, I will give you a ready-made audience to guarantee your success* (see Matt 4:1-11). Would Jesus define success according to the world's standards of size and numbers, or according to the kingdom of God standard of a life-changing relationship?

Growing up in North America, surrounded by a culture of affluence, we often make certain assumptions about what it means to be a Christian. These assumptions easily translate into conditions we set for how God is to operate. Without even realizing it, we fall into the sin of dictating how God should provide for us, care for us, and cause us to be successful. Instead of nailing this selfish nature to the cross, we dictate the terms for how God should attend to it!

As we help people understand what it means to go from living under the control of a sinful "I" nature to finding their identity in Christ, Paul's words guide us. "For Christ's love compels us, because we are convinced that one died for all, and therefore all died. And he died for all, that those who live should no longer live for themselves but for him who died for them and was raised again" (2 Cor. 5:14-15). Jesus' love compels us and his model of giving himself for others sets the standard. The choice is clear: Will we live for self or for him who died for us?

After years of sacrifice and paying their dues, Howard and Linda were beginning to see the benefits of their hard work. They had found a great neighborhood, an excellent school system, a church where they felt at home, and a comfortable house where they would raise their two kids. Their marriage was strong and the kids were flourishing. Howard and Linda had no idea how much their lives would change in the next six months. A routine physical led to an MRI which revealed a tumor. The preliminary tests suggested a worst case scenario: Howard had perhaps months to live. Within three weeks, their world went from idyllic to devastating.

Howard described the time of waiting for the final results of a complicated biopsy as the most intense experience of his life. Parts of his day were spent on his face crying out for healing, consolation, and a sustaining grace. Other parts of his day were dedicated to spending as much time as possible with Linda and their two young children, whom he realized he might not have the opportunity to raise. Early one morning before sunrise, Howard was pleading with God to spare his life for the sake of his kids. Howard had grown up with an absent father and longed to provide his kids with the love, attention, life lessons, and opportunities he had missed out on with his own dad. They were so young and needed him so much; he could not bear the thought of not being there for them. As the tears poured out, Howard became very aware of God's presence. And then Howard experienced his heavenly Father's love in a way he never had before. He heard God say, "You now have a glimpse of the relationship I long to have with my children who don't know me."

After a week that felt like a year of waiting, the news came back. The tumor was in a dangerous location in his brain, but it was benign and could be treated with medication, not surgery or radiation. A worst case scenario suddenly changed to a best case scenario.

It took Howard and Linda months to process all that happened during those several weeks. One thing they knew for sure, their lives would never be the same. According to Howard, "There is something about facing your mortality that puts life into perspective." The picture of standing before God to give an account of how he had invested all his material, relational, and spiritual gifts was sobering. It was time to start living in a way that was consistent with how they believed. It was time to start living with an eternal perspective.

 Pause to Consider

Imagine yourself listening to Howard and Linda share their story. Where and how do you join them in this unfolding drama? One way of organizing all this rich material is by using the 3 P's of listening.

1. Listen for what is **Painful**. Howard talked about the physical pain of living with an undiagnosed brain tumor for several months, the pain of not being able to raise his kids, and eventually getting a glimpse of the Heavenly Father's painful longing for his lost children. Linda described the pain of losing her soul mate, the intense pain of not knowing if she could trust God, and the pain of what this would mean for their kids.

2. Listen for the **Protest**. At the root of every protest lies a "should." Howard and Linda spent the first fifteen years of marriage in low-paying ministry jobs and going back to school for advanced training in order to better serve God. They watched their peers get established in successful careers and start families. Now it was finally their turn. They had faithfully done their part, now it was up to God to do his. Howard and Linda, like most of us, had expectations about how life circumstances and relationships were supposed to work. One of the most powerful lessons they learned from their experience was the degree to which they had been dictating to Holy God the terms of the relationship! While they protested, God lovingly and mercifully revealed the "non-negotiables" they had carried into the relationship.

3. Listen to determine if they go to the **Place** of painful memories. Howard's days and nights were filled with Jacob-like wrestling matches as he grasped for some understanding of why God would let this happen. During these times of thrashing he encountered

Holy Spirit-prompted moments of decision. Would he fill up on a sustaining grace or slide into his Inner Room? His Inner Room was filled with his own father wounds, guilt over not being more productive for God, and a host of "what-ifs" for the future of his family. Linda stayed solid throughout the several-week process, but experienced her Inner Room crash after the good news of a benign tumor was delivered. Even though the news was the best case scenario, all her expectations about how God protects were obliterated. Her Inner Room now had a whole new section focusing on the questions: "Is God safe?" and "Can he be trusted?"

Within six months of receiving the devastating news, Howard and Linda were working with a Christian organization that was devoted to spreading the good news of a Father's love, care, and guidance to his children. Howard summarized the change with these words, "The 70% cut in pay and the 50% reduction in the square footage of our home allow us to enjoy a 100% increase in our ability to invest in the lives of people who want to get to know the God we met while on our faces. We've never been happier."

It took a life-threatening tumor for Howard and Linda to make the shift in their "I" from self-preservation to kingdom of God investment. What will it take for the people you are helping to make this shift? To enable their "I" part to fulfill its God-ordained potential, we need to take the people we are helping to the place where the corrupted "I" makes its last stand. This place is called the Inner Room. This is where we store and rehearse our mistakes, failures, disappointments, broken promises, and "what ifs." In other words, the Inner Room is the place where we store the things about our lives we most dislike and the non-negotiables we are unwilling to release.

Every day we choose to define ourselves in one of two ways: according to the truths of who we are in Christ or according to the lies coming from our Inner Room. Following is a practical and powerful tool for showing individuals, step-by-step, what the Inner Room is stealing from them and how to confront its lies.

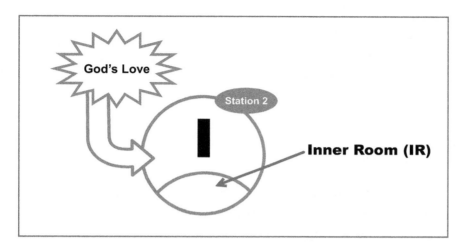

I. Start with what sends you to your Inner Room. Check all that apply:

_____ *Painful memories from the past*

_____ *Not being appreciated or treated the way I think I should be*

_____ *Rejection*

_____ *Criticism*

_____ *Frustration in my important relationships*

_____ *Comparisons to others who seem to have everything going for them*

Each checked response provides an example of how our enjoyment of life can get hijacked by a reminder of what we feel is wrong or missing. The people you are helping may check several, or even all, of the options, showing you just how strong the pull of the Inner Room is in their life. I have even had some individuals tell me that they do not go to their Inner Room; they live there. The next section helps identify the feelings that accompany a visit to the Inner Room.

II. When I go to my Inner Room, I often feel:

_____ *Guilty*
_____ *Lonely*
_____ *Unfairly treated*
_____ *Insecure*
_____ *Like giving up*
_____ *Disappointed with myself or others*
_____ *Angry*
_____ *Vengeful*
_____ *Other*

Are you getting a sense of how destructive this place is to us? It not only steals what is pleasant, it convinces us that we are victims without hope of things getting better. At this point in your discussion, it is usually helpful to have individuals describe what their Inner Room looks like. What events or interactions are playing on the big screen? What conversations are on a continuous feedback loop? Who are the main characters in this drama and what are they saying? Some individuals become quite elaborate in their descriptions. When you sense they are fully in their Inner Room, move to the next step and ask them what they do there.

III. What I do there:

_____ *Fill up on sadness*
_____ *Replay the hurts*
_____ *Get frustrated with what is wrong with me, my family, friends, school, work, etc.*
_____ *Remind myself that others can't be trusted*
_____ *Fantasize about escapes such as becoming extremely successful so others will recognize how incredible I really am*
_____ *Wait until someone comes to rescue me*
_____ *Find ways of manipulating people into meeting my needs*
_____ *Other*

The responses to the "what I do there" options are helpful in determining how deeply the person goes into their Inner Room. If they are going in deep, staying there for long periods of time, and even developing strategies for what to do while they are there, their Inner Room identity is probably much stronger than their identity in Christ. Be patient, because it may take some time for a shift in identity to occur. While the shift in identity is underway, the next section provides a helpful way of monitoring and confronting the potentially destructive thoughts and responses associated with these feelings.

IV. Identify the destructive thoughts and responses coming from the Inner Room's toxic fuel:

_____ *Stay very busy in order to avoid any meaningful reflection (anesthesia of busyness)*

_____ *Don't get too close to anyone who could see the real me*

_____ *Get angry with the people who have not treated me well*

_____ *Think about how much better life would be if only ......*

_____ *Criticize others in order to keep the focus away from me*

_____ *Become involved in doing good things, but with unhealthy motives*

With a contorted face and tears flowing, Tom described the stupidity of his affair and how it tore apart his family and led to divorce. He was sorry for the pain his infidelity had caused his wife, but his deepest ache came each night as he thought about the bedtime routine of stories, prayers, and hugs he was missing out on with his young girls. It was clear that Tom was living in his Inner Room and it was taking him under. The exhaustion of working two jobs to financially support two households wasn't helping. Tom reported that the hardest part of the day was in the evening after a full day of work. Because his second job was more brawn than brain, there was too much time for his thoughts to replay his failures as a husband and father. His Inner Room was fully operational, replaying over and over the memories of a lifetime of abusive relationships.

Finally Tom decided it was time to begin taking his thoughts captive. He asked the Holy Spirit to prompt him when his thoughts turned in a negative direction. Tom returned for our next visit with this report: "As soon as my shift started, I thought about my girls and felt a familiar sadness creep in. I started to fill up on the sadness as it drew me into my Inner Room. I guess it was the Holy Spirit who helped me catch myself before going in too deep. I focused on unloading the truck and was fine for about twenty minutes before the 'I can't believe how stupid you were' thoughts entered. They took me right into my Inner Room and were joined with reminders of all the other mistakes I've made. With God's help I battled my way out." Tom went on to describe the mental exhaustion he felt after an entire night of doing battle against his Inner Room. I was shocked when he said, "After eighteen trips into my Room that night, I lost count." He went on to say, "The next night was a little easier and by the end of the week, I could tell right away when I was heading there." Tom declared war on his Inner Room. Here are some suggestions that helped him.

V. Fighting against going into the Inner Room

For starters, encourage the people you are working with to start recognizing when they are heading to their Inner Room and to say out loud, "I have a <u>choice</u> whether to go here or not." If they are already in the Inner Room, they can say out loud, "I have a <u>choice</u> to stay here or exit." (For comic relief, they will want to observe the reactions of those within hearing distance!) Acknowledging that they have choices is a helpful first step toward breaking the feeling of powerlessness. If they have a choice to go to or stay in the Inner Room, then they also have a choice not to go in or not to stay.

While they are in their Inner Room, they may want to ask themselves:

- Does coming to this place help?
- How much of my life is controlled by this place?
- Is there another way of living that is free from this place?

Gradually, with the promptings and empowerment of the Holy Spirit, they can make the choice to exit the room quickly or, better yet, to not go there at all.

In the next chapter, we will explore what the Redeemer wants to do to set us free from the destructive influence of this Room. You might be shocked by what God wants to do with its contents.

Reflection Questions:

1. What are some examples of provision, care, or success issues that cause people to seek help?

2. What are some ways we are at risk for using the spiritual gifting / resources God has given us for our own personal comforts or to get our emotional needs met?

3. How many of our prayers reflect an incorrect expectation of how we think God is supposed to provide, care, or cause success?

4. What is your reaction to Howard's and Linda's story?

5. How often do you go to your Inner Room? What are some of the triggers that send you there? Are you aware of what you think / do while you're there?

Chapter 6

A LIVING SACRIFICE

Station 2 Continued

If the Inner Room is such a destructive place, why do we go there and fill up on all the toxic memories and messages? Why would we want to be exposed to so many lies about who we are and be reminded that we are victims of our past? Most of us would argue that we do not want to be there, listening to those messages. But why then do we find ourselves returning over and over to this place of discouragement? One reason we may go there is because, even though we know the Inner Room is not a helpful place for us to be, it is still a familiar place. We have spent so much time there that we have grown accustomed to the lies and we find a measure of comfort in their familiarity. Unfortunately, in some cases we have actually taken the worst ingredients of this place and used them to fashion an identity for ourselves.

To be totally free from the Inner Room and its influence on us, we need to do more than just avoid going there. We need to clean out the Room! To do this, we must become a Living Sacrifice. This term comes from Paul's letter to the Christ-followers in Rome. At a critical juncture in his correspondence with them, Paul wrote, "Therefore, I urge you, brothers and sisters, in view of God's mercy, to offer your bodies as a living sacrifice, holy and pleasing to God— this is your true and proper worship" (Rom. 12:1).

What does it mean to be a living sacrifice? At first consideration, the two words seem to present an oxymoron. How can something be given up as a sacrifice—which in biblical language meant it was killed, burned, or in some way destroyed—and still live? Might Paul be suggesting that the attitude we carry in our journey toward Christ-likeness should be that of a sacrifice with no rights, no option to climb off the altar in protest about how we are being offered? Might he also then be suggesting that with this identification as a sacrifice, we live our lives in whatever way God directs as our spiritual act of worship?

Yes to all of the above! Throughout his letters to the early communities of faith, Paul gave specific guidelines about what it means to present ourselves as Living Sacrifices. Through these guidelines, Paul showed us three main areas of his "I" part being brought to the altar and given to Jesus.

First, Paul brought his very best to the altar. We find this in his letter to the Philippians. Before his conversion, Paul's heritage, his zeal for his cause, and his high standing in the religious community put him in elite company (see Phil. 3:4-6). Paul was talented and dedicated, but he misused these qualities. These are the kind of traits which, if not surrendered, can easily become a source of pride. The only way to prevent this from happening is to follow Paul's example. "But whatever were gains to me I now consider loss for the sake of Christ. What is more, I consider everything a loss because of the surpassing worth of knowing Christ Jesus my Lord, for whose sake I have lost all things. I consider them garbage, that I may gain Christ and be found in him ..." (Phil. 3:7-9).

Often, we hang on to what we consider to be our best qualities because we need others to recognize and value them as much as we do. When they do not, our pride is hurt, our ego is bruised, and our desire to associate with those people is greatly diminished; in other words, lots of material for the Inner Room.

The second thing Paul brought to the altar was his very worst. We can only speculate about the degree to which Paul struggled with his past mistakes, but he did mention them in several of his letters. In his letter to the Corinthians he wrote, "For I am the least of the apostles and do not even deserve to be called an apostle, because I persecuted the church of God" (1 Cor. 15:9). To his young apprentice Timothy, he said, "Even though I was once a blasphemer and a persecutor and a violent man, I was shown mercy because I acted in ignorance and unbelief.... Here is a trustworthy saying that deserves full acceptance: Christ Jesus came into the world to save sinners—of whom I am the worst" (1 Tim. 1:13, 15). Paul had the choice to let the memories of his violent attacks on Christ's followers haunt him, or to bring those memories to the altar with all of his other shortcomings and failures.

Some may question whether Paul holding on to the memories of his past mistakes would really be such a bad thing. Might not those memories serve as a type of motivational fuel to propel him in his missionary journeys? We might not call it a form of penance, but perhaps holding on to the memories could be an indicator of his desire to atone for past regrets. There is no question that people throughout the history of the church have accomplished significant works for God because they were motivated by this type of fuel.

In your work as a helper, you will no doubt encounter some similarly zealous workers for God whose toxic fuel contaminates their ministry. A fuel that requires us to be constantly reminded of our past failures eventually does harm to us and others. Paul recognized his need to remove the toxic fuel of past mistakes when he wrote, "Brothers and sisters, I do not consider myself yet to have taken hold of it. But one thing I do: *Forgetting what is behind* and straining toward what is ahead, I press on toward the goal ..." (Phil. 3:13-14, emphasis added). The contents of the inner room, accompanied by all their lies and condemnation, must be removed and brought to the altar as a representation of our very worst!

The final ingredient Paul brought to the altar was his current condition. In his second letter to the Corinthians Paul described a personal experience that is somewhat hard to grasp. Paul had a vision of something he called the "third heaven" where he heard inexpressible things that man is not allowed to tell. What made this experience so complicated was that it was accompanied by a "thorn in [the] flesh," a "messenger of Satan, to torment [him]" (see 2 Cor. 12:1-7). Over the span of fourteen years, on three separate occasions, Paul unsuccessfully pleaded with the Lord to remove this thorn. Here was Paul's current condition being brought to the altar. He received a vision beyond description, but with it came a physical limitation that added to the already difficult travel of his missionary journeys. In addition to the physical hardship was the emotional confusion over receiving a beautiful gift from God that came with terrible strings attached. Paul, who was used to having his prayers for others answered, found that these prayers for himself went unanswered. This must have caused some moments of spiritual questioning. Paul's current condition contained a mixture of physical, emotional, and spiritual difficulty as he brought it to the altar.

Sacrifices require more than just an offering on the altar. They also require someone at the altar to receive the sacrifice. Ask those you help who they envision at the altar. This is an important next step. The image of who is at the altar greatly influences their motivation for going there. If their image is of a frustrated, disappointed, or angry God, the person will likely be hesitant to approach him. When this is how we see God, we naturally want to make our offering more acceptable before presenting it. Some of the best work you do as a helper may be helping individuals develop a more biblically accurate picture of who waits for them at the altar. The Bible, as God's autobiography, is filled with crucial images that show how he wants to be known to his people. Here are a few examples:

- Comforter in sorrow (see Jer. 8:18)
- Strong deliverer (see Ps. 140:7)
- Prince of Peace (see Is. 9:6)

- Redeemer (see Ps. 19:14)
- Great high priest (see Heb. 4:14)
- God of all comfort (see 2 Cor. 1:3)

One of the images that provides considerable encouragement is found in Jesus' story of the prodigal son. The son in the story is returning home after squandering his inheritance. The father, who represents God, sees the son while he is still a long way off. To the amazement of the listeners, the father, filled with compassion, does not even wait for the son to come to him, but instead runs to the son, throws his arms around him and kisses him (see Luke 15:18-20). Could it be that Jesus does not even wait for us to reach the altar but instead runs to us with open arms and embraces us? What a hopeful picture for those weighed down with years of accumulated guilt.

Surprising as it may seem, some individuals have trouble receiving the warm and accepting embrace of God. An ongoing refusal to be loved is one of the most difficult conditions to overcome as we help others along their journey. In my imagined picture of Jesus, I can easily see his persistence on display with these individuals, as he puts his arms around his hesitant followers and leads them to the altar. Since most of us are better at giving than receiving, Jesus asks what they would like to present as their living sacrifice. They reluctantly offer their very best. In his presence, they now recognize that what they prized looks putrid by way of comparison to his love, but amazingly he still asks for and receives it. They hear him ask if there is anything else. Very reluctantly they answer "Yes, but nothing that has value." He says, "I will determine what has value, why don't you give it to me?" With a mixture of shame and embarrassment, they offer their very worst. To their amazement, he takes it as if he had a use for it. Seeing this, even before he asks, they present their current condition as the final offering in their Living Sacrifice.

Now that Jesus has it all, as is required of a sacrifice, they notice him turning to a huge cauldron at the altar. Carefully he begins mixing their very best, their very worst, and their current conditions into the cauldron. There is a smile on his face as he enjoys watching the recipe come together. It is a recipe that was established for each of us while we were being knit together in our mother's womb (see Ps. 139:13). Jesus proclaims that these are the necessary ingredients for developing a man or woman of God, and with words that cause decades of heaviness to fall from their shoulders, he announces, "There are no unusable ingredients in the recipe!"

Sarah was a well-spoken twenty-two-year-old who struggled with a paralyzing guilt. She ended one of our sessions by saying, "I need some time to allow the 'no unusable ingredients' idea to sink in." Sarah returned two weeks later. The idea of ingredients mixing together was understandable, but how the Inner Room junk from her past could have value was not making sense. I saw this as a great opportunity to continue our discussion of Philippians 3, specifically, verse 10 when Paul said, "I want to know Christ." I invited Sarah to know the Christ who was at the altar as her Redeemer. Paul continued with what it is that he wanted to know about Christ: "the power of his resurrection." Sarah now began to connect several key concepts. Most importantly, for the first time in her life she began to understand that there is no force in the entire universe, other than Christ's resurrection power, that could take the shameful ingredients of her Inner Room and transform them into something that has eternal beauty and significance. That is why he is called the Redeemer. Sarah also began to understand why she was so drawn to working with high school girls. The resurrection power of Christ allowed her to use the lessons she learned from living her own painful mistakes to effectively relate to the girls in her small group who struggled. She was the first small group leader in the church who was able to connect with this challenging group of girls.

Pause to Consider

It was difficult for Sarah, like many others, to get her mind around the idea of "no unusable ingredients." In order for this concept to make sense, she had to revisit her understanding of the unchanging, unconditional, and totally comprehensive nature of God's love. Generally speaking, Sarah knew Jesus as the redeemer for sins, she just hadn't considered how personal and specific he wanted to be with her.

One of the most enjoyable moments in working with people is when a Holy Spirit-illuminated truth from God's Word connects with them in a deeply personal way. One of the mistakes I've made during these sacred moments is to start babbling like Peter at the transfiguration of Jesus. A more appropriate response would be to hit the pause button and allow some time for the significance of what just took place to be absorbed. For Sarah this meant taking a step back in order to consider what being loved like this really meant.

Her hesitation raises a common question asked by many helpers, "Why would someone think twice or even refuse to be loved?" Two typical answers are "I don't know if I can trust it" and "I'm too unworthy to receive it." My hunch is that exposure to perfect love produces an unsettledness because it demands a response. It forces the issue of what we are going to do with our very best, very worst, and current condition. For some, the offer of perfect love is met with a readiness to surrender all the ingredients. For others, there is a willingness to offer a few ingredients to see what God does with them. And finally for others, there is no movement toward the altar because they must remain in control of the ingredients and the recipe. Helpers are not put off by the responses of hesitancy or resistance, they patiently move forward with an appreciation that these too are vital ingredients in the recipe.

When Sarah realized that the worst parts of her life were now being used to make a difference in the lives of others, she became even more energized. A few weeks later she reported reading a devotional on Romans 8:1 which says, "Therefore, there is now no condemnation for those who are in Christ Jesus." Another "light bulb" moment occurred. Because all the ingredients in the Inner Room have been mixed into the recipe, they no longer exist in their previous state. Therefore, there is nothing left to condemn her. Sarah was becoming a testimony of how the truths of God's Word really do set people free.

As her work with the adolescent girls continued, Sarah had the opportunity to experience the rest of Philippians 3:10. She was now learning what it meant to know Christ through sharing in the fellowship of his sufferings. Despite her investment in the lives of these girls, several continued down a destructive path. Sarah saw it coming and with all her love and prayers did everything she knew to try to prevent the painful consequences that awaited the girls. As she did, Sarah realized for the first time how much it must grieve Jesus to watch his children refuse his love. Through her tears, she said, "It hurts to see where they're headed." I reassured her that this is what it means to share, in our own way, a small piece of the suffering of Jesus. I also reminded her that the destructive patterns of the girls, much like her own, were not beyond the redemptive touch of Jesus. They would become painful ingredients, but they could still be an important part of the recipe.

Once the Inner Room has been exposed and its contents are being transformed, our true identity in Christ can begin to grow stronger. Appendix D provides a verse-by-verse narrative of who we are in Christ from the first five chapters of Ephesians. The truths in the appendix can be used for individuals, couples, or groups. Individuals are encouraged to read over the list at their own pace as often as necessary to allow the truth to sink in. Based on experience, you may want to tell them to allow several readings, mixed with time for meditation, before what is being read takes hold. The truths that are most difficult to receive become the springboard for future discussions.

Appendix D also can be used to speak truths over one another. One of the most powerful exercises my wife and I do on couples' retreats is to have each husband say his wife's name and then read a truth about her identity in Christ. We have come to realize how deeply many wives have longed for their husbands to speak biblical truth into their lives. The exercise is then repeated as the wife speaks her husband's name followed by a reading of his true identity in Christ. After this exercise, the climate of the retreat changes as couples begin to realize that one of the best gifts they give their marriage is a clean Inner Room and a healthy identity in Christ.

Reflection Questions:

1. In Paul's model of what it means to be a living sacrifice, he brought his very best, very worst, and current conditions to the altar to be mixed into the recipe. What are your very best, very worst, and current condition ingredients?

2. As you bring these ingredients to the altar, what is your image of who is at the altar ready to receive your living sacrifice offerings?

3. Sarah had trouble grasping the "no unusable ingredients" concept until she saw how some of her worst ingredients were being used to benefit others. Think about how some of your difficult experiences have been used to help you help others.

4. Appendix D offers a biblical perspective of our true "I" identity in Christ. As you read the verses from Ephesians, which ones speak to you most profoundly at this point in your journey? What is it like to place the name of your spouse or close friend at the beginning of the verse and speak these truths over them?

Chapter 7

Movement into the "We"

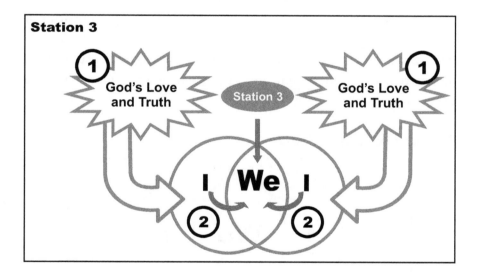

God's love and truth from Station 1, having saturated the "I" part in Station 2, now begin to overflow into the "We" of Station 3. This is where most couples, like Justin and Megan from chapter 2, want to begin their counseling. I asked Justin and Megan to put the "We" work on hold, because one of the most important lessons I learned from my early mistakes as a couples' counselor is that the best "We" growth occurs when Stations 1 and 2 are working well.

As you can see from the diagram above, there are now two circles (individuals) coming together to form a relationship. These overlapping circles produce a "We" that represents the emotional, physical, intellectual, recreational, and spiritual intimacies that go into a meaningful relationship.

Understandably, the amount of time available to spend cultivating one's "We" relationships will vary from day-to-day, month-to-month, or even season-to-season. Relationships have their ups and downs and can move between healthy and unhealthy, depending on the circumstances and the time that the individuals are devoting to their mutual growth. One of the first steps in beginning "We" work is understanding what healthy and unhealthy "We" relationships look like. Couples will be able to diagnose the condition of their relationship by comparing it to the five examples that follow. The five types of I/We overlap are: 1) harmonious balance, 2) seeing each as roommates, 3) feeling suffocated, 4) experiencing need without love, or 5) having one willing and one resistant partner.

1) Harmonious Balance

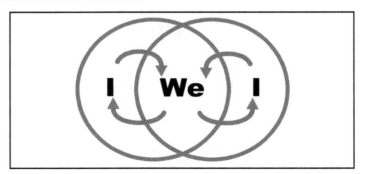

A balanced relationship occurs when two healthy individuals feed their "We" together. All the spiritual and personal growth work done up to this point in Stations 1 and 2 has prepared these individuals to love each other out of the overflow of all the positive experiences and thought patterns developed in those first two stations.

One of the paradoxical truths found in Jesus' teachings about relationships is that the more we give, the more we position ourselves to receive. In other words, as we selflessly allow God's love and truth to flow through us to another person, we create a bond with that person from which we receive the encouragement and freedom to continue our "I" growth. This type of balance creates a dynamic growth potential as "I" pours into "We." A strong "We," in turn, promotes continued growth in the "I."

2) Roommates

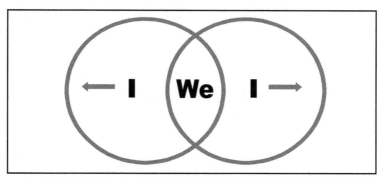

Two individuals living with a malnourished "We" find themselves functioning more like roommates than close companions enjoying the benefits of an intimate relationship. If you find yourself helping a couple living as roommates, you will want to explore why their "We" is so malnourished.

One of the most common causes for a shrinking "We" is a reluctance to deal with conflict on the part of one or both individuals. Relationships by their very nature are designed to experience conflict. Two individuals are never going to see every situation the same way or see the same solution to every problem that confronts them. Conflict is inevitable and not something we should be afraid of or seek to avoid. On the contrary, resolution of these conflicts is an important catalyst for building trust. Unless a couple learns how to resolve their differences, their growth together is stunted. Each unresolved issue becomes a building block that creates a barrier between the couple. Over the years, the building blocks begin to form an impenetrable wall blocking the flow of intimacy to a "We" that gradually becomes starved for attention and affection. It's only a question of time before one individual's heart grows cold and one individual's mind begins to entertain what life would be like away from the other person.

Another common cause of a malnourished "We" is the demands of life. Managing a home, establishing and maintaining a career, and raising children can appear to require all of one's time and energy. Over time, these couples go from being lovers, to co-laborers, to distant roommates. Couples living as distant roommates are often getting their primary emotional needs met through their work and kids. While work and kids are important investments of our time, if we allow them to provide the emotional connection we should be getting from our "We" relationship, they quickly become the plugs discussed in chapter 1. For some, a painful wake-up call comes as the last child prepares to leave home or as career pursuits become unfulfilling. Couples who find they are living as roommates need not despair. While it is not easy to shift from years of living as roommates to becoming intimate partners, it can be done.

3) Suffocated

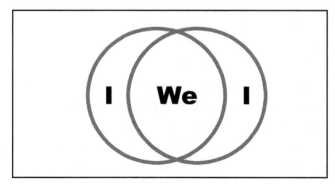

The third type of I/We overlap reflects an unhealthy focus on the "We" that doesn't allow the "I" to develop. When the "I" is not cared for, it begins to shrivel up. Because a depleted "I" has little to offer, the "We" then becomes stagnant. A depleted "I" also puts pressure on the other person to provide what should have been replenished from personal time spent in Stations 1 and 2.

Describing this degree of overlap as suffocating can be confusing because the large "We" may appear to be an accurate representation of the goal established by God for man and woman to become one flesh (see Gen. 2:24). Becoming one flesh, however, does not mean losing one's "I" part and its true identity in Christ. Instead, I believe it speaks more to being a good steward of the "I" in Christ while remaining completely available for one's spouse.

When the "We" takes over and begins to crowd out each partner's "I," pressure begins to build at the center of the relationship. This kind of pressure suffocates partners and sets them up for the impossible task of trying to provide for each other what can only be supplied by God.

4) Need, not Love

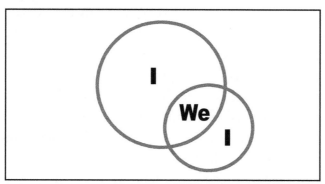

In some relationships, one of the parties has more power and control. When this happens, the dominant partners use their "I" space, not for personal growth, but for selfish pursuits. Either gender is capable of assuming the dominant role. The following example shows what can happen when it's a male.

Chuck described his bachelor days as wide open. His motto was "work hard, play hard," which he did with a group of thrill-seeking buddies. As some of the group members began to settle down, Chuck found himself spending more time with Virginia. It was Virginia's first serious relationship. Since her own social life was practically nonexistent, Virginia was delighted with whatever attention Chuck gave her. After a couple of months of dating, she interpreted his request to live together as an opportunity for her world to open up. As they were soon to find out, Chuck's expectations were drastically different.

It didn't take long before Virginia found herself in direct competition with the guys for Chuck's time. Her romanticized notions about their future life together were gradually replaced with a resignation that it was her role to make sure Chuck's world worked. This went on for about six months until one day when Virginia had coffee with her best friend. Her friend simply asked, "What happened to the Virginia I used to know?"

Virginia mustered up the courage to talk with Chuck about the direction of their relationship. Chuck was a very intelligent man in all areas of his life except for relationships. His ability to talk about relationship issues could best be described as underdeveloped. Not surprisingly, Virginia's attempts to talk about their relationship were unsuccessful. Fortunately for Virginia, a few close friends helped her recapture her "I" and walked with her as she learned how to love Chuck enough not to allow his destructive relationship patterns to continue. After several months of pleading, arguing, and finally giving him an ultimatum, Chuck very reluctantly agreed to come in for counseling.

If, as a helper, you encounter a "Chuck," avoid making any suggestions for change or pointing out what's being done incorrectly during the initial visit. Emphasize that this is not a time for either partner to build his or her case, blame, or attack the other person. It is a time for non-defensive dialogue and personal reflection.

The more verbal person, in this case Virginia, may need to be given guidelines for how much to share. Too much relational information, shared too quickly, can be overwhelming. Since relationship concepts were not a part of Chuck's vocabulary, I drew a diagram of overlapping circles to summarize what I was hearing them both communicate.

As a helper, you may find it necessary to communicate to people with a variety of different learning styles. An auditory person will be fine talking for an hour. Others may need word pictures or metaphors. Because I knew Chuck enjoyed hunting, I quickly made a comparison between the patience needed for duck hunting and the patience required to work through different expectations for a relationship.

A visual person, often the male, may benefit more from one diagram than an hour of talking. When I introduced the five "I/We" overlapping circles, Chuck became much more involved in the discussion. Looking at the diagrams, Virginia expressed that her ideal was a combination of the balanced "We" and the suffocated "We." Chuck had never thought about what a relationship should look like. He was simply copying what he had observed from other men in his family. As he studied the different diagrams, Chuck initially concluded that his relationship with Virginia was most like being roommates, but after further consideration, Chuck began to see himself as the big "I" of the need-based relationship. This was a turning point for Virginia and Chuck. Without admitting it, Chuck was communicating to Virginia his desire to maintain a pre-relationship lifestyle with the guys (his large "I" space), while also having a place to land when he wanted his affection needs met (a comfortable "We" space that was run according to his terms). In essence, he was expecting Virginia to make sure her "I" was dedicated to creating the physical and emotional safe haven he could enjoy at his discretion.

What caused Virginia to lower her standards of how to be treated in a relationship and accept a position in the little "I" space? Virginia acknowledged that she allowed Chuck to convince her that this was as good as it would get for her. She also confided that, even at the lowest points of the relationship, it still felt good to be needed. That is why this condition is referred to as a "need, not love" relationship. Virginia needed to be needed, while Chuck needed lots of space for his pursuits and an emotional safety net.

Helpers should approach "need, not love" relationships with great caution. Chuck finally came around, but plenty of others do not. They greatly resent any attempts to alter a situation that allows them to maintain maximum personal freedom, no accountability, and emotional security all in the same relationship.

 Pause to Consider

What motivates someone to seek help? Is it some form of physical or emotional pain? Perhaps a destructive lifestyle pattern needs to be altered. For many, living with unresolved relationship problems is a strong motivator. Virginia's emotional pain and Chuck's lifestyle choices were strong motivators for her, but not for Chuck. Here's the challenge in getting started with relationship counseling: rarely do both parties agree on the severity of the problems or on the timing of when to seek help. I can appreciate how hard it is for guys like Chuck to ask for help with something they don't even recognize as a problem. If they do recognize that there is a problem, it is way out of their comfort zone to ask for help with something so personal. Whether it is a reluctant spouse, a rebellious adolescent, or a Christian leader facing church discipline, when someone is coming to see you because of an ultimatum, give careful consideration to how you get started. A mistake I've made on several occasions was trying to sell this person on the advantages of getting help. I wanted to convince them of all the benefits of a better marriage, home life, or work place. I soon realized the error of wanting something more for them than they wanted. Another mistake I made, under the pressure of not knowing how many visits I was going to have with a person, was trying to cram ten sessions worth of help into two. The lesson learned is anytime I'm working harder than the person who has the problem, I'm not really helping.

Instead of trying to convince resistant or non-motivated individuals that they needed help, I began asking myself, "What is preventing them from wanting to, or being able to talk about what is happening in their relationship?" When I shifted the discussion away from *what* was wrong with Chuck and Virginia's relationship to *why* it was so hard to talk about it, five reasons emerged. Chuck described 1) being tired of hearing about his failures and shortcomings; 2) being convinced that he could never measure up to Virginia's expectations; and 3) really having a hard time talking about anything when she became emotional. Virginia added that it was very difficult to make any headway because of 4) the pressure she felt to communicate her words correctly the first time or risk having Chuck get frustrated and walk away; and 5) the fear of saying something that would hurt Chuck's feelings and cause him to shut down and withdraw from her.

It was easy to see how the degree of "I/We" overlap was affected by these conditions. The good news for Chuck and Virginia, and many other couples, is that when the manner in which they discuss their relationship problems changed, there was no longer any resistance to having those conversations.

Women in the small "I" are sometimes equally difficult to help. In some cultures, girls and young women are taught that their role in life is to make sure their husband's world works for him. Some even teach this as a form of biblical submission. While submission is definitely a biblical concept, the Bible defines it as the mutual giving of one's self for the well-being of the other person, not a destructive pattern of one individual getting his/her needs met at the expense of the other person.

Another way to help "need, not love" couples develop a healthier relationship is to talk about the concept of stewardship. Within the context of a lifetime commitment, both individuals should assume the responsibility to provide the conditions necessary for their partner to thrive. They may even find it helpful to envision a scenario where God announces, "It is time to return the spouse who was on loan to you," and to think about the condition in which God's precious child will be given back to him.

5) Willing I, Resistant I

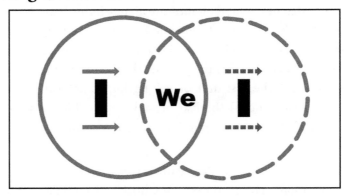

One of the most painful relationships to witness is the willing "I," resistant "I." One person is willing to work on the relationship, while the other, for a variety of reasons, is not. My heart goes out to the pursuers whose attempts to reconcile are met with responses of "I'm not interested," "You're the one with all the problems," "If you weren't so …, then maybe things could be different," or "You knew I was this way when we got together, don't try to change me now."

At some point in the counseling process be prepared for the willing person to ask, "How long should I pursue?" I wish there were an equation that could calculate pursuit measured against resistance to determine the probability of a person changing. Since there is not, my counsel is to make either decision, to continue pursuing or back off, based on prayerful discernment and lots of love. If led to continue reaching out, then I believe God will provide a sustaining grace to keep going. If led to halt the pursuit, then I believe God graciously empowers the former pursuer with a tough love that says, "I will no longer support or enable destructive behavior." Either decision made in love allows the willing person to remain in a state of receptivity if the resisting party has a change of heart.

If you are helping a willing "I," resistant "I" couple, you should be aware of a twist that sometimes occurs in these relationships. On a number of occasions, I have witnessed a resistant person become repentant and turn back toward the willing partner, sometimes after years of hard-heartedness, only to find, to everyone's shock, that the once willing partner is no longer interested. The best term I can use for this turnabout is a "Therapeutic Backfire." If you find yourself rejoicing over the softening of a resistant partner, you may want to reassure the willing partner that it is sometimes surprisingly difficult to accept and gradually begin to trust a change of heart.

Now that you have helped the couple you are counseling identify the status of their relationship, you need to know how to help them build a spiritually strong foundation in their "We." We will look at that next, by exploring one of the most important commands Jesus gave about how to get along with others.

Reflection Questions:

1. Which of the five types of "I/We" overlap have you experienced or observed?

2. What are some of the risk factors contributing to a potentially malnourished "We"?

3. What are some other suggestions for how to help a couple living in a "need, not love" type of relationship?

4. What are some possible reasons why the willing "I" would refuse the reparative attempts of the formerly resistant "I"?

5. Which of the five types of overlap do think would be the most difficult to help?

Chapter 8

THE SPIRITUAL FOUNDATION FOR THE "WE"

One of the basic beliefs of the Christian faith is that God has always existed in three persons - Father, Son, and Spirit. How they exist as three, yet one, reveals something significant about their nature. From the point of creation to eternity past, they enjoyed the indescribable intimacy of a perfect love relationship. Imagine the contrast Jesus experienced between the loving embrace of the Father and Spirit versus the insults and pain of sin-ravaged people when he came to live among us. Jesus' healing presence and personal sacrifice were life-giving displays of the Father's love to this fallen world. By coming to earth Jesus provided windows through which we catch glimpses of truths that cannot be fully grasped by finite minds. The windows are framed with three powerful teachings which form the core of what it means to be a follower of Jesus.

- "Love the Lord your God with all your heart and with all your soul and with all your mind and with all your strength" (Mark 12:30). Jesus begins by making sure we understand the totality of a love relationship with God. Loving God requires complete dedication.
- "… Love your neighbor as yourself" (Mark 12:31). This verse teaches us that God's love always has an outflow to others.

Jesus said this second command to love others was like the first command to love God. When we love God completely, that love will overflow into love for others.

- "My command is this: Love each other as I have loved you" (John 15:12). This verse affirms the importance of loving others. But then it goes on to add that we must first receive from Christ what we will give to others.

In order to fulfill the command to love others as we have been loved, first we must explore how Jesus loves us, and then we can make his love the model for how we love others. The box below provides eight examples of how Jesus loves us.

Examples of How Jesus Loves Us

1. He **pardons** us: *Greater love has no one than this, that he lay down his life for his friends* (John 15:13).

2. He **prunes** us: *He cuts off every branch in me that bears no fruit, while every branch that does bear fruit he prunes so that it will be even more fruitful* (John 15:2).

3. He **passes on** what he knows: *I no longer call you servants, because a servant does not know his master's business. Instead, I have called you friends, for everything that I learned from my Father I have made known to you* (John 15:15).

4. He **pursues** us: *You did not choose me, but I chose you and appointed you to go and bear fruit—fruit that will last—and so that whatever you ask in my name the Father will give you* (John 15:16).

5. He **pervades** our hearts with joy: *I have told you this so that my joy may be in you and that your joy may be complete* (John 15:11).

6. He **protects** us: *I will remain in the world no longer, but they are still in the world, and I am coming to you. Holy Father, protect them by the power of your name—the name you gave me—so that*

---

they may be one as we are one. While I was with them, I protected them and kept them safe by that name you gave me. None has been lost except the one doomed to destruction so that Scripture would be fulfilled (John 17:11, 12).

7. He **provides** what we need: *Remain in me, as I also remain in you. No branch can bear fruit by itself; it must remain in the vine. Neither can you bear fruit unless you remain in me. I am the vine; you are the branches. If you remain in me and I in you, you will bear much fruit; apart from me you can do nothing* (John 15:4, 5).

8. He **penetrates** our fearful places with his peace: *Peace I leave with you; my peace I give you. I do not give to you as the world gives. Do not let your hearts be troubled and do not be afraid* (John 14:27). *I have told you these things, so that in me you may have peace. In this world you will have trouble. But take heart! I have overcome the world* (John 16:33).

These verses reveal a God who expresses his love in a variety of meaningful ways. How well are you able to receive and live in these personal expressions of his love? The depth of our spiritual journey is determined by the degree to which we allow ourselves to be loved by God.

The eight ways God models his love for us also provide a pattern for how to establish a spiritual foundation in our "We" relationships, fulfilling Jesus' command to love as we've been loved. Let's go through the eight examples and consider how to help others apply these truths. As you help others, be sure to monitor how well they are receiving God's various expressions of love before they try to extend love to others. Also be prepared for the opportunities you will have to model these truths in the context of the helping relationship with its occasional misunderstandings.

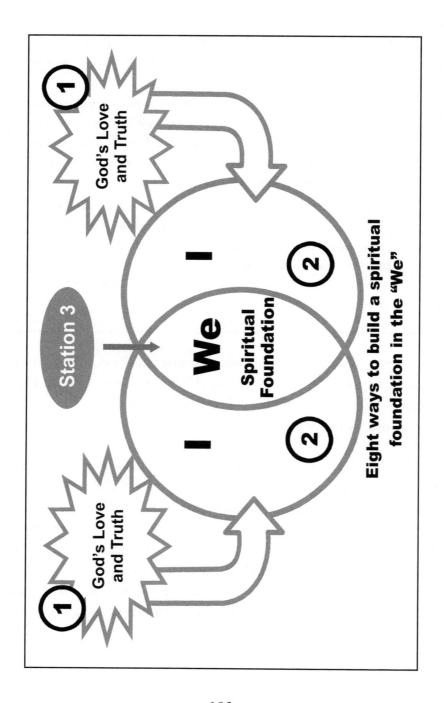

Only God can **pardon** individuals of their sin, but we can pardon or extend forgiveness for the wrongs committed against us. This is an important concept that we will cover in greater depth in chapter 10. For now, you simply want to help others understand that a solid "We" relationship is only possible when individuals are able to forgive each other as they have been forgiven by God. In his parable of the unmerciful servant, Jesus had some very strong words for the man who had his enormous debt cancelled by the master, but then turned around and threw into jail the man who owed him a very small debt (see Matt. 18:23-35).

God loves us enough to **prune** us. It's important to remind those we are helping that the purpose for God's pruning is not to punish, but to prepare us for more growth. One of the most dangerous misconceptions portrayed by Hollywood is the notion that if we find the right person, the relationship will be effortless. On the contrary, the most significant "We" relationships require a willingness to prune and to be pruned. Whether we like it or not, God chose intimate relationships to be his workshop.

For example, if I view marriage as God's workshop, then I can expect my spouse to be given the precise tools needed to work on me. It seems only natural that this person will force me to face things in my life that have been hidden or that are unpleasant. The list of possibilities is long: selfishness, pride, possessiveness, fear of incompetence being exposed, laziness, blind spots, etc. As long as my life is under the influence of these paralyzing or destructive forces, God's work in and through me is limited. I can get frustrated with my spouse for forcing me to face my weaknesses, or I can thank God for the redemptive process that transforms my exposed weaknesses into displays of His grace. Similarly, when I see a weakness in my spouse, I can choose to focus on my spouse's deficits, or I can ask God to fill me with the love that will allow me to engage in a respectful discussion about what needs attention. Each time I receive the grace to make a positive choice in that moment of decision, a part of me becomes more like Christ and the relational workshop is accomplishing its goal.

Because learning how to give and receive feedback is such an essential part of what takes place in the relational workshop, I strongly suggest that before any lifetime commitments are made, people think long and hard about whether their potential partner has the interest and ability to engage in this kind of honest dialogue. Next to a heart for God, the most significant quality to look for in a lifetime partner is a teachable spirit. For those already in a committed relationship and struggling, one of the most powerful catalysts for turning a relationship around is a blend of humility and a willingness to receive feedback.

A final word about how to help others take advantage of this significant concept addresses the importance of how and when to prune. When our children were toddlers, Susan and I decided she would be a stay-at-home mom. This was a blessing for both our kids and us as parents. However, as any mother of young children would agree, there are days when work away from home has some appeal. When I returned home one evening, I couldn't help but notice a large pile of clippings at the curb. They were from what used to be a six-by-eight-foot privet bush. As I looked around the corner of the house, I saw a one-by-one-foot stub. When I carefully inquired about her day, Susan informed me that she had learned a very valuable lesson. The kids were having a cranky day and she needed a break. When they went down for their naps, she went outside for a moment of sanity and noticed how overgrown the privet had become. What started out as a little shaping turned into a massacre. Susan wryly said the built-up frustration was wonderfully released as the clippers took off another limb. Her valuable lesson: "It's not a good idea to prune when frustrated." We've tried to honor that lesson in our relationship.

It's difficult for me to comprehend the magnitude of Jesus' willingness to **pass on** everything he's learned from the Father to us. Jesus' attitude provides a stark contrast to the organizational leadership model that equates information with power. Those in the control seats offer only as much information as each person needs to fulfill a specific responsibility. Jesus' promise is to offer as much information as we can handle. The only limitation is our capacity to receive. How would our close relationships change if both parties were committed to passing on the lessons being learned in Stations 1 and 2, even the messy ones that are still in progress? Jesus made it a regular practice to share his inner world with others during both private and public encounters. Appropriate transparency communicates a desire to bring as much helpful information into the "We" as possible. When that self-disclosure is welcomed and received well, intimacy grows.

What does it mean to **pursue** someone you've already caught? Fortunately for us, Jesus chose to pursue and keep pursuing. The opposite of pursuing is taking someone for granted. Susan and I have led a number of growth groups for newlyweds to help them get off to a solid start. One of the questions we like to ask is, "How has the pursuit of your spouse changed since the first few months of dating?" For most, there has been a considerable drop off. The follow-up question is, "If this pattern continues, what will the degree of pursuit look like after five or ten years of marriage?" Taking those closest to us for granted is one of the fastest ways to devalue them, yet we do it on a daily basis. If we remain true to Jesus' command to love others as God loves us, then we will find as many creative ways as possible to say to our spouse or closest friends, "I choose you to be a treasured priority in my life."

Pervade conveys the idea of filling up or saturating, and this is exactly what Jesus wants to do with an outpouring of joy in our hearts. Joy is not a word I hear many people use to describe their everyday lives. Of course, if it were they probably wouldn't be coming in for counseling. Honestly, if someone appears to be too joyful, I become somewhat suspicious. It seems to be more helpful to consider joy less like an emotion and more like a choice of perspective. What a wonderful gift we offer those closest to us when our presence has the perspective-altering effect of helping them refocus on what is most pleasant in life. What a joy for us to be able to pervade the hearts of those we love with the joy that comes from an outpouring of God's love.

Protection is often associated with the commitment to prevent any physical harm from taking place. The context of Jesus' words certainly implies his commitment to keep his disciples physically safe while he was with them. However, there also appears to be another type of protection being requested. Jesus prays for the oneness of our relationship with the Father and the Son to be protected. Jesus feels so strongly about protecting this intimacy that he calls upon the power of God's name to be the defending force that prevents any competing affections from creeping in. How strongly do we feel about protecting our relationships? How do we protect them and what are we protecting them from? How many emotional affairs, or worse, begin as an innocent search of a past boyfriend or girlfriend's activities and appearance on Facebook? In an attempt to recapture the glorious possibilities of youth, our hearts and minds entertain only the positive memories of these past relationships. What started as curiosity soon violates the promise of emotional exclusivity.

Using Jesus' example, we see that the best way to protect our oneness comes through intercessory prayer. In a selfless demonstration of how important the other person is to us, we bring everything we know about who they are and what they need before the Father as often as we can. Our selflessness also extends to doing everything we can to promote the sense of oneness Jesus talks about in his prayer.

How committed are we to the growth of those we care about? Jesus' formula for growth is simple, "I am the vine; you are the branches" (John 15:5a). As the vine, Jesus **provides** everything necessary for the branch to flourish, or in his words, to bear much fruit. As the vine, Jesus established a natural growth process that proceeds from a right relationship. In the first ten verses of John 15, Jesus uses the word "remain" eleven times. When we love others as he loves us, we commit to providing a relational environment that encourages them to reach their full potential.

As mentioned earlier, Susan stayed home with our kids when they were young. She provided a wonderful environment for our children to flourish. Because of all she was pouring out for the kids, her "I" part was beginning to shrink. On three different occasions during the stay-at-home years, we decided it was important for her to get an evening away on a weekly basis. She chose to take evening courses in areas of personal interest. The coursework provided a refreshing change of pace and some much appreciated adult interaction.

Loving someone enough to provide what they need also includes deliberately finding ways to bring out their untapped potential. Sometimes this requires giving the other person the freedom to fail, having patience as the other person explores new ways to use their gifts and abilities, removing restrictions, and being willing to walk with the other person as they clean up previous mistakes or heal emotional wounds from the past. Unrealized capabilities begin to surface when we love another person well enough to become a relational safe harbor.

The final demonstration of love that builds a strong spiritual foundation for the "We" is found in Jesus' promise to **penetrate** our fearful places with his peace. As Jesus prepared his disciples for his departure from this world, he took the traditional greeting of peace and expanded it to include a promise that the Holy Spirit would soon come and quiet their troubled hearts and replace their fears with his peaceful presence. Since perfect love drives out fear (see 1 John 4:18), the only things we have to fear are those we have yet to surrender to the love of Christ. When we love as we have been loved, we can expect to encounter the fearful, yet-to-be-surrendered places in others. When this happens, will we pull away or take the opportunity to love well a person whose heart is troubled?

The foundation for all future work in the "We" is set. The need for having such a strong foundation of love will become even more apparent in the next chapter as we guide others in how to handle their conflicts.

Pause to Consider

How many of Jesus' teachings were given in response to relationship problems, whether brought on by cultural prejudices, abuses of authority, family squabbles, or jealousy? Jesus made sure his disciples received the formal teaching they needed, but he also paid very close attention to how well it was being applied in their day-to-day life together. These were men with strong personalities living in close proximity, experiencing physical hardships, trying to make sense of their Rabbi's unorthodox subject matter and methods. It was like living in a pressure cooker. As the time for Jesus' departure grew close, the opposition intensified and the teachings turned dark. Can you feel the edginess among the disciples that caused them to turn on each other and to begin making comparisons about who was more important? Instead of coming together, the group was beginning to unravel. Jesus took advantage of this teachable moment to remind his disciples how well they had been loved in each of these eight areas. Jesus wanted them to know without any doubt, "You don't have to worry about not getting your fair share. There is an unlimited supply of love that I enjoy providing for each of you. The very personal ways I give it to you will become your frame of reference for how to give it to others." In the next few months the disciples would go from hearing this promise, to believing it, to finally experiencing it. It would radically change how they treated each other and would compel them to share this Good News with others.

Refection Questions

1. Take some time to reflect on specific ways God has loved you in each of these eight categories. Which are easiest / hardest to receive from Him?

    _____ Pardons us

    _____ Prunes us

_____ Passes on what he knows

_____ Pursues us

_____ Pervades our hearts with joy

_____ Protects us

_____ Provides what we need

_____ Penetrates our fearful places with his peace

2. Now take some time to reflect on how well you are fulfilling the command to love as you have been loved. Where are you doing well? Where do you need some improvement?

3. What are the differences between a relationship that has a strong spiritual foundation and one that does not?

4. List an area where the Holy Spirit has recently been pruning you. What are you learning about how the Holy Spirit prunes? What are you learning about your receptivity to being pruned by the Holy Spirit or others?

Chapter 9

THE CRITICAL PAUSE

Station 3 Continued

Key Verses that Discuss Conflict:

Prov. 15: 1   A gentle answer turns away wrath, but a harsh word stirs up anger.

Luke 6: 45   Out of the overflow of the heart the mouth speaks.

Eph. 4: 26   Be angry, but do not sin.

James 1: 19   Let every one of you be quick to hear, slow to speak, and slow to anger.

Put yourself in the following scenarios:

- You are waiting patiently in traffic to exit the highway at a busy interchange. As the cars inch along, a late model sports car cuts right in front of you, barely missing your front bumper.
- Even though your spouse did not come through with the help she promised, you finally finished a major home renovation project. You are feeling very proud of the results. Your spouse comes home and never notices that the project is complete. When you call to her attention the finished product, she comments, "It's about time."

- You're driving in your car listening to your music when you hear a song that resurrects strong feelings from a previous relationship. Memories of the hurt or regret overtake you.

Whether we see them as triggers that get pulled or buttons that get pushed, certain events, statements, and memories generate a reaction inside of us to which we naturally respond.

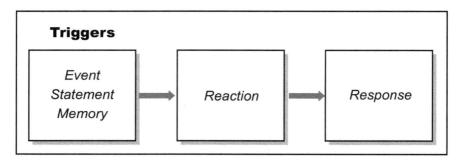

An **event** *trigger is an unpleasant interaction with someone or something.* In addition to the situations previously mentioned, events can include things like the kids leaving their bikes in the middle of the driveway, the neighborhood dog barking all night, a major repair job improperly done, a committee member dominating a meeting with irrelevant information, or a politician from an opposing party making outlandish claims. You get the idea. Sometimes we call them pet peeves. They are the things that get us worked up and are hard to let go.

A negative **statement** *is something said to or about you that triggers strong feelings inside.* Negative statements can take the form of put-downs, critical comments, and sarcasm. Because these words sting, they are often met with defensiveness, counter attacks, or withdrawal.

Memory *is a powerful trigger because the mind replays the negative events or statements.* Memories are included as triggers because they have a great impact on our moods. Replaying an event or statement in our minds easily produces the same negative feelings. In some cases the memory may be even more powerful because we have had time to embellish it.

Ask the people you're helping to identify some of their specific triggers. Are they more susceptible to events, statements, or memories?

Triggers, by definition, produce a reaction. Emotional triggers initiate the "fight-or-flight" rush of energy that comes from our central nervous system. This is the body's way of preparing us for what comes next. Imagine yourself enjoying a pleasant evening with friends when unexpectedly the conversation turns to an embarrassing story about one of your past mistakes. Typically, you have a good-natured disposition that allows you to laugh at yourself. Not tonight. The way the story is being told, who is telling it, and the insinuations about your absentmindedness are not sitting well. An event, words being said about you, and embellished memories have pulled all your triggers. The churning in your stomach and the throbbing in your head warn you that the reaction is intense. Some decisions must be made quickly, or you run the risk of responding in a way that will do relational damage.

What determines how people react and then respond to the triggers in situations like this? Why do some people go into a rage when they are cut off in traffic, while others laugh it off? Why do some friends stuff their frustrations, while others always seem to be itching for a good argument? It is easy, and even comforting, to be able to categorize our reactions, to say someone responds a certain way because she is a "Type A" personality or he has an "ABCD" temperament. Labels provide a way to bring legitimacy to what we do. Unfortunately, they also provide a "that's just the way I am" excuse for unregulated emotions and irresponsible behavior.

Perhaps there is another explanation for why we react and respond the way we do. We each have a set of beliefs about the way we should be treated. Examples of our beliefs include: drivers should be courteous, bosses should notice and appreciate our contributions, spouses should know what we need and be eager to provide it, and good friends shouldn't require too much from us.

These "shoulds" become the control panel of buttons that get pushed. Getting close in a relationship is risky business because sooner or later the other person will find our control panel. It is amazing to see how skilled some people are at finding and pushing these buttons.

Can you appreciate the liability of having a control panel full of expectations? If our sense of well-being is determined by how others treat us, people who may not care about us, or even know us, are determining how we feel about ourselves.

Jason readily admitted he had problems controlling his temper. His outbursts had cost the company two good salespeople and damaged the relationship with an important customer. His boss put him on notice that it had to stop. His company even paid for him to attend an anger management seminar where he learned some helpful exercises for stress reduction. Jason reported that the seminar helped him cut back on the number of outbursts, but the ones that did come out were even more intense than before. We began by identifying his significant "We" relationships at work. We then made a list of potential triggers in these relationships. The next step was hard for Jason, but with some coaching, he was able to monitor what was going on inside (his reaction) when he was triggered.

We next made a list of the work-related "shoulds" that were setting him up to be triggered. For example, Jason said one of the recent blow-ups came at a staff meeting when several members of the sales team had not completed their quarterly reports. Jason identified the "should" behind his trigger as an expectation that people should be responsible enough to get their work done on time. Jason was surprised when I said, "I agree." I also threw him a curve when I said, "Your problem is less about anger, and more about poor communication. If you have something important to say, let's help you find a better way of expressing it."

I told Jason that it was time to stop focusing on how others should be responding to him and time to begin taking responsibility for controlling his own attitudes and responses. Any response that is based on a reaction will usually get us into trouble. If our goal is healthier responses, then something needs to happen to break the reaction-to-response sequence.

The Critical Pause is the solution. It becomes the adult version of a "time out" and is our way of pausing the interaction long enough to cool down and regain perspective. A Critical Pause not only protects the relationship, it is also one of the best investments of time I know. Would you rather spend ten minutes regaining perspective by taking a Critical Pause or spend several days doing damage control after making an inflammatory response?

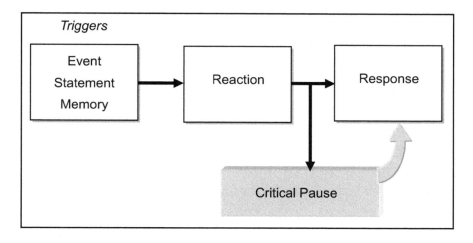

How do you initiate the Critical Pause? In a one-on-one setting, you let the other person know you need some time to regroup. In a group or professional setting where taking a break is not appropriate, you need to buy yourself some time by shifting the focus to something less threatening until you're prepared to make constructive responses about the difficult issue.

If you stop talking or walk away without communicating your intentions, you are probably treating yourself to a good pout. Pout-and-Chase is a favorite game for some couples. As the pouter withdraws, the chaser pursues in order to make everything better. Pouting is a form of manipulation we use to get our own way. It's a habit the chaser can help break by no longer chasing. Pouting without someone chasing is miserable. Trust me, I know!

In order to avoid any appearance of pouting, individuals who call for a Critical Pause should also offer a time when they anticipate being ready to resume the discussion. One husband gave me a look of incredulity and questioned why he would want to resume a heated discussion after things finally calmed down. His wife's response was, "That's why we never resolve anything." The strategy for dealing with our disagreements is not to ignore or minimize them, but to engage in a respectful dialogue about what's bothering us. In Ephesians 4:26 Paul instructs us not to sin in our anger, suggesting that we "do not let the sun not go down while [we] are still angry." His point is that if parties in conflict don't learn how to recover quickly, the resulting festering resentment does considerable harm.

What do you do during the Critical Pause? This is where it gets difficult. Even individuals who understand the importance of quickly stopping a heated discussion don't always know what to do next. A misuse of the Critical Pause occurs when people use the time to build better rebuttals and gather more ammunition. *If used correctly, the Critical Pause allows us time to seek God's help in generating an attitude readjustment.* This includes accepting personal responsibility for whatever part we may have played in the disagreement. That is hard to do, especially when our beliefs about how we should be treated are violated.

How do we readjust our attitudes? Let's review Jesus teaching, "Why do you look at the speck of sawdust in your brother's eye and pay no attention to the plank in your own eye?" (Matt. 7:3) As suggested previously, a loose paraphrase of this teaching might read: Before addressing someone else's behavior (a speck), examine the condition of your heart (a plank).

One of the reasons an attitude readjustment is so difficult is that it requires us to operate in a manner that is not natural to us. Instead of trying to get our own needs met, defend our "shoulds," or prove that we're right, an attitude readjustment helps us find ways to respect and connect.

Emotionally and spiritually strong people will accept responsibility for whatever part they may have contributed to the conflict and even be able to explore why their triggers are getting pulled. In Jason's case, his reactions were triggered by legitimate concerns such as the need to follow procedures and meet goals. Through some insightful reflection in an extended Critical Pause, he also realized that some of his anger was triggered by the realization that several of his close friends from college were climbing the corporate ladder much more quickly than he was. These comparisons were creating an underlying frustration that spilled out in his harsh responses. By using the Critical Pause, Jason was able to break the pattern of unhealthy responses and identify why he was being triggered so easily.

Jason experimented with an approach that focused on connecting before correcting. By connecting with what was going on inside of him, he was able to adjust his expectations. At the same time by connecting better with his staff, he was able to respond more effectively when his expectations weren't met. During one of our sessions Jason described a tool he began using in his Critical Pause. When the pressure would start to build, he would pull out an index card. It read, "The goal is to excel in sales, not paperwork. A failure to meet deadlines is not a personal attack on me."

These adjustments allowed Jason to eliminate three major triggers. Not surprisingly, his more relaxed approach opened up opportunities for more social interaction. Jason realized that with the improved relationships, he could still work on staff development, but now it was done more privately and respectfully. Only one member of the team resisted his efforts to connect. This person's attempts to stir up dissension lost steam and he eventually left for another company.

Pause to Consider

As soon as Jason sat down for our first visit he began unloading his pent-up frustrations about the incompetence of his staff, the lack of support he received from his boss, and the ever-changing company policies and procedures. One area of frustration led to another, and then to another. Jason was in a free fall with no parachute. After about fifteen minutes I suggested a pause. The mentally-disorganized and emotionally-charged way Jason presented his problems gave me a hint of what was going on inside, and it wasn't pretty. Jason needed an internal spreadsheet for where to put everything. Without some kind of internal structure, he would just keep spinning without finding any traction. One way to help Jason organize his internal chaos was to draw out a Critical Pause Flow Chart. We started with the areas of frustration and concern that were providing the Triggers, moved to the Reactions, and finally explored his current choice of Responses.

Potential Triggers	Internal Reactions	External Responses

- Relationship with boss
- Relationship with sales staff
- Policies and procedures
- Career uncertainty
- Financial pressure at home
	- Increasing stress / worry
	- A desire to tell people off
	- Heartburn
	- Fantasies about working
	  for the competitor
		- Blow up in anger
		- Complain
		- Become less tolerant of staff
		- Put out feelers for who
		  was hiring

With the flow chart in hand, Jason was able to bring order to his jumbled up thoughts and emotions. With this many important Triggers in play, Jason realized that each day he was being hooked by at least one, and often several of these issues. We then agreed that the Reactions were understandable, but not okay to act on. By using his Critical Pause he would begin taking responsibility for choosing an appropriate Response, instead of allowing one to flow out of a Reaction, which is rarely helpful. There was much work to do, but we now had a new way of looking at Jason's patterns and prioritizing which parts to address first.

Jason's successful "We" work was complemented by the spiritual growth he was experiencing in Stations 1 and 2. After having a few months to consolidate his intense period of growth, Jason made an insightful comment, "Any situation that forces me to rely on Christ's help instead of my natural tendencies is growth-producing."

As helpers present this model to others, one question that often gets asked is, **"How do I know when I'm ready to exit the Critical Pause and resume the discussion?"** Two simple questions will guide this decision. The first: "Are you still interested in who is right or in how to win the argument?" If the answer is yes, then resuming the discussion will only start the next round of the fight. The second question: "Do I want to use the upcoming discussion as a way to foster a better relationship?" If the answer is yes, then I am seeing the big picture of how God is using the "We" workshop to teach me important lessons about myself and to equip me with the ability to work through relational conflicts well.

One husband who was learning how to practice the Critical Pause summarized his experience with these words: "As my wife and I try to put this marriage back together, I encounter moments of decision several times each day. During these moments I am faced with the decision to turn toward or away from her. When I turn toward her, I walk into a grace that gives me exactly what I need to love well."

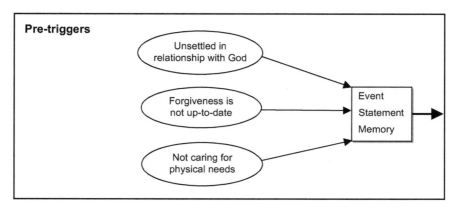

When individuals find themselves moving through the triggers-to-reaction-to-response cycle often and with intensity, you will want to consider what they are doing or not doing that is causing this. Pre-trigger conditions are one potential cause for this pattern.

Each of these pre-trigger conditions can affect how we react when one of our triggers is pulled. It is worth spending some time exploring how to get these important areas working well for us.

In the next chapter we will concentrate on the pre-trigger of forgiveness, which plays such a huge part in how well our "We" works that it requires some in-depth attention.

Reflection Questions:

1. How easily "triggered" are you? Are you most easily triggered by an event, statement, or memory?

2. Jason used an index card with some reminders to help him with his attitude readjustment. What are some strategies (e.g., reading certain Bible passages, meditating, taking a walk, etc.) you can employ to help gain perspective?

3. If you are having trouble making an attitude adjustment and exiting the Critical Pause in a timely manner, what other factors may be affecting you? Some examples might be a deeper unresolved issue or a feeling like you always have to be the first to seek reconciliation.

4. Which of the pre-triggers do you need to monitor the most?

5. Jason made a list of his workplace "shoulds." Identify the place(s) where you are regularly triggered (at home, at work, while driving, with certain friends). What are some of the "shoulds" you're living with in these situations?

Chapter 10

THE FORGIVENESS MARKER

Station 3 Continued

One of the most soulful men I've ever worked with in therapy said, "I forgave her after the first affair. I will not forgive her for having a second."

Nate had moved out of the house and for six months lived with a mixture of relief and anguish. A year later he came back to see me. The divorce proceedings were nearing completion, but the anguish was unbearable. He said, "I know I can never live with her again, but I also know that at some point I've got to forgive her." I asked why he knew he had to forgive her. Nate described a series of encounters with Jesus. In his despair he would sit in a vacant church and cry for help. During one of his visits, he began staring at a cross. For the first time in his life the reality of what Jesus had done penetrated his heart. Every sin he had ever committed was covered with the blood of Jesus. I expected his conversion would produce a long-awaited peace. Instead, he felt trapped. Nate now knew that because of what Jesus had done for him, he must extend forgiveness to his unfaithful spouse, but he couldn't. I asked what was preventing him. In one of those moments of spiritual clarity he replied, "If I forgive her, I can no longer keep my anger. If my anger is gone, she will re-enter my life. If she re-enters my life, I will be deeply hurt. I cannot go through that again!"

Nate had experienced Jesus' forgiveness of his sins. He understood that forgiveness was God's way of initiating a very personal relationship. But how forgiveness was supposed to work in the context of intimate and sometimes hurtful human relationships was unclear. He was confused over what seem to be conflicting teachings about forgiveness in the Bible. Matthew 18 is a good example. In verses 21-35, Jesus instructs his followers about the importance of unlimited forgiveness. On the surface, the teaching of unlimited forgiveness seems to contradict the earlier teaching (vv. 15-20) of excommunication for the unrepentant member of the group. In one teaching Jesus seems to be saying there are no limits to forgiveness. In the other teaching he seems to draw a line that, when crossed, will break our fellowship with him. You can see from this passage how one's ideas about forgiveness depend on which verses are selected. To help simplify what is often a very confusing concept, I have developed the "Forgiveness Marker."

Choosing to forgive another is a monumental task, so it seems appropriate to mark the point in time when this happens, to create a monument that reminds us of this pivotal moment. Planting a Forgiveness Marker signifies that we are inviting God to do a cleansing work in our lives.

Similar to the Old Testament accounts of people erecting monuments or altars to acknowledge God's powerful intervention in their lives, we are marking our entry into the process of forgiveness. One of the best examples of creating a monument to acknowledge God's faithfulness is found in Joshua 4. Joshua commanded one man from each tribe to take a stone out of the place where God parted the Jordan

River. They were instructed to place the stones on the Promised Land side of the river to create a memorial to God's deliverance that would stand for generations. "[Joshua] did this so that all the peoples of the earth might know that the hand of the LORD is powerful and so that you might always fear the LORD your God" (Josh. 4:24).

At a given point in time, you choose to plant a Forgiveness Marker as an act of faith that declares your desire to let go or release what you are holding against someone. A refusal to forgive carries consequences, one of which is not having control over your own well-being. If you are waiting for someone else to take responsibility for how they hurt you, and they don't, you are left holding onto the painful consequences and memories. As you wait for this person who is either unsuccessfully trying to make amends, or who could care less about your hurt, you are saying, "I can't be okay until you do something to make it better." Under these conditions, who is in control of your well-being?

Once you decide it's time to plant the Forgiveness Marker in the present, you are ready to address the accumulated hurts from the past.

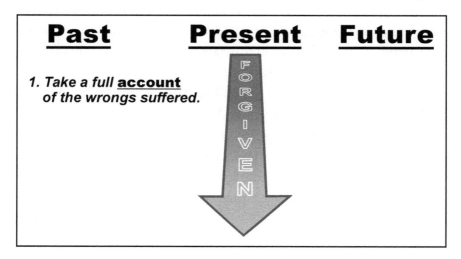

The first step in facing past hurts is to take a full account of the wrongs suffered. Resistance in taking this step sometimes comes from an unwillingness to dig up past hurts. As a helper, you may hear statements like, "It's best to let sleeping dogs lie." The hope is that the hurts will lessen with time. The reality is that unless forgiveness has occurred, those past hurts become an unwelcome part of our identity.

Another reason for resistance is an unwillingness to dishonor or criticize the people who inflicted the hurt, usually parents. Helpers may hear statements like, "The Bible teaches us to honor our parents. I don't want to say anything bad about them." "They were doing the best they could." "When I consider how other parents treated their kids, I didn't have it so bad." The purpose for taking a full account is not to launch an attack on parents or even to assign blame. It is to acknowledge that what occurred was painful and to understand how it affects who we are today. Ignoring, minimizing, or spiritualizing past hurts forces us into an artificial world where pain must be avoided. If we are not free to embrace that pain and to invite the presence of Christ to redeem it, we will go through life as victims.

Sometimes we resist taking a full account because we believe the painful experiences were deserved. Distorted thinking suggests that the harsh treatment or neglect was justified because of personal deficits or a failure to measure up to imposed standards. In this case, if we are not careful, taking a full account of wrongs suffered actually fuels the memories of perceived failure.

Some individuals mistakenly think that taking a full account means dredging up every painful event and reliving it. A more constructive approach is to identify categories of wrongs suffered without getting hung up on specifics. Since the process is not about assigning blame, accuracy about events in the distant past is not essential. (Situations where there was abuse or significant trauma would, however, require a different therapeutic approach.) Examples of categories of past hurts include: a partner's unfaithfulness, emotionally or physically absent parents, mistreatment by siblings, phony Christians, or unfair treatment by employers.

Past	**Present**
1. *Take a full account of the wrong suffered.*	F O R G I V E N
2. *Grieve the* **hurt** *or* **loss.**	

Have you ever prayed to forgive someone, but still had trouble letting go of what happened? Doubt surfaces as to whether your prayer was sincere. Perhaps it was hard to let go because you never spent time grieving the hurt or loss. Instead of whitewashing what happened or pretending it was no big deal, we have already taken an honest account of the wrong suffered. The honest accounting is then followed by an admission of how much it hurt or what was lost.

As Michelle shared her life story with the group, she paused to regain control of her emotions as she recounted her after-school ritual of riding the bus home in silence, praying that maybe today her mother would be sober. Michelle was working on step 2 of the Forgiveness Marker. She would eventually reach a point of being able to forgive her mother, but currently she was grieving the things alcohol had stolen.

Some individuals try to minimize their hurt by suggesting others have it much worse. As a helper, you should remind them that this is not a contest to see who has been hurt the worst. Regardless of where their experience falls on the pain continuum, acknowledging its effects is an important step in forgiving the person who caused it. It also validates the experience by giving it the weight it deserves.

Jesus certainly did not take lightly the past sins of all humankind when he prayed in the Garden of Gethsemane the night before his crucifixion. He was grieving what sin had done to separate people from their loving heavenly Father. He also was painfully aware of what it would cost him to go from having never experienced sin to becoming the embodiment of it (see 2 Cor. 5:21) so that a broken relationship could be restored. In Psalm 22, David prophetically described the inner monologue Jesus had as he grieved these losses.

Following Jesus' example is helpful because he demonstrates the difference between feeling pain and grieving. Unfortunately, many people feel pain, but do not grieve. Many young adults spend years feeling the loss of never receiving what they wanted from their parents. What is the difference between feeling the hurts or losses and grieving? Grieving is a way of providing an outlet for our pain. In Jesus' final hours he found outlets for his grief through a final meal with his closest companions, a powerful teaching on the importance of serving one another, an honest expression of feelings to the Father, and an invitation for a repentant sinner to be with him in Paradise.

Fred was a hard-working accountant struggling with the pain of a divorce. His ability to express what was going on inside was nonexistent. Instead of brooding at home in his empty house, Fred decided to distract himself and take an evening class to help him upgrade the computer network for his employees. Registration for the class was full. Desperate to get his mind off the divorce, he signed up for the only class that fit his schedule. It was a ceramics class. The accountant now had an outlet. All the pain that had built up over the past several years was flowing through his fingers into the clay. He worked the clay, threw pots (not against the wall), fired and glazed them. He found an expression for his pain that allowed him to grieve as he created.

Consider some of the best works of art, literature, or music. They are often masterful expressions of pain that found an outlet through a process of grieving. When the grieving process is underway, our pain is expressed, discussed, and sometimes creatively displayed on canvas or through music, physical exertion, acts of service to those who are hurting, or journaling.

One of the primary benefits of grieving is that you don't allow the pain to get stuck inside. When the pain of deep hurts and significant losses is owned and expressed, the forgiveness process can move forward.

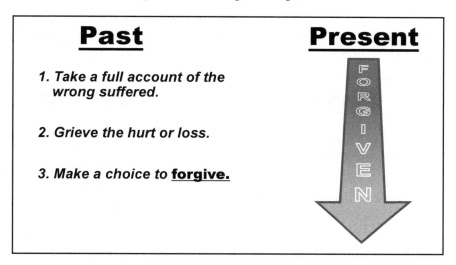

Making a choice to forgive (step 3) is a powerful decision; it's just not the best place to start the process. The offer of forgiveness is most meaningful when we've acknowledged and grieved what is being forgiven. After taking a full account of the wrongs suffered and grieving the hurts and losses, we now make a deliberate choice to forgive—to release or let go. Making the choice to forgive in step 3 provides the release we had hoped for because it combines our willful commitment with our emotional healing.

Having made the choice to forgive, we can now move to step 4 where we let go of any expectation for restitution. It's great if offending parties recognize where they've caused hurt and even make some attempts at restitution. But what happens when they don't? The process of forgiveness may come to a screeching halt if the offer of forgiveness is contingent on another person's actions. While we wait for them to take action, our sense of well-being is held captive. Making a choice to forgive and letting go of any expectation for restitution only works if we do so unconditionally. Going through steps 1 – 4 does not require the cooperation or even the participation of the offending parties. We are guided through the forgiveness process by the healing love of Christ until we experience the freedom from our past that only he can provide. No longer are we on hold as we wait for someone to give us what we hope for. No longer are we intimidated by their haunting threats.

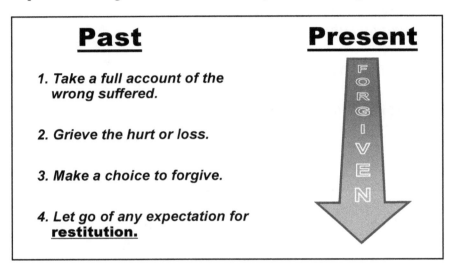

Past   Present

1. **Take a full account of the wrong suffered.**

2. **Grieve the hurt or loss.**

3. **Make a choice to forgive.**

4. **Let go of any expectation for <u>restitution.</u>**

F
O
R
G
I
V
E
N

Consider the Critical Pause model of chapter 9. Notice that one of the pre-triggers was not having our forgiveness up-to-date. Let's imagine a couple has just experienced a misunderstanding in their "We." Some sarcastic words were spoken (a trigger). Frustration is building (a reaction). What do you think is going to happen with the unresolved hurt from the past? I can hear the back-up siren of the huge dump truck, ready to drop its load of past frustrations and hurts onto this argument. Now the couple is sitting in a mound of garbage from the past. What is the likelihood of them being able to successfully resolve their current disagreement while sitting with the reminders of previous hurts? The dump truck of past hurts must be driven to the landfill where it can be buried. When the garbage of the past is no longer affecting them, this couple will have a much better chance of resolving whatever current issue they are facing.

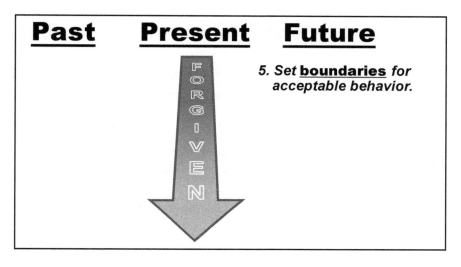

If I forgive someone, do I have to continue the relationship? This was the question raised by Nate at the beginning of the chapter. Another way of asking the question is, "If I forgive the past, am I required to pursue a future relationship that may repeat the hurtful patterns?" The answer is, it depends. By advancing through steps 1 – 4 on the past side of the marker, individuals are preparing themselves to re-engage with a fresh start. (Situations where there has been some form of abuse would be an exception.) If both parties are willing to establish healthy guidelines or boundaries for acceptable behavior going forward, the future relationship has promise. Unlike the unconditional nature of forgiveness for the past, a future relationship depends on a willingness to change destructive ways of relating. Setting negotiated boundaries for acceptable behavior also offers the protection of a "go slow" mechanism while trust is restored.

David's relationship with Saul is a perfect example of forgiving the past but not going forward with a relationship in the future. In 1 Samuel chapters 24 and 26 we read that David is running for his life from the malicious Saul. On two occasions David has the opportunity to kill his nemesis, but he refuses to raise his hand against God's anointed. What a great picture of someone who trusted in God's timing. When Saul realizes David spared his live, he confesses his sin and invites David to come home with him. David extends forgiveness but does not enter into a future relationship with Saul. Why not? Remember that David had years of experience watching how quickly Saul could turn against him. *Confession must be followed by true repentance that is measured over time.*

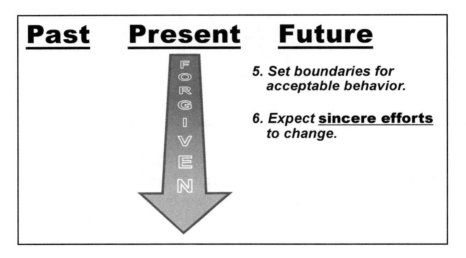

If appropriate boundaries are established and honored, there will be sincere efforts to change. Note the emphasis on efforts, not perfection. Steps 5 and 6 provide the means to educate others about how to have a relationship with us. The feedback is given lovingly and respectfully but firmly and is accompanied by a willingness to receive feedback about what adjustments may be required of us.

If the individual's efforts are short-lived then we have some hard decisions to make about the future of the relationship. We may choose to distance ourselves from this person, but what happens when they are a spouse, family member, or close associate? In such cases creating physical distance may not be an option. Their lack of effort to follow through on previously discussed terms communicates that this relationship is no longer a priority for them. We may wish to honor their decision by allowing emotional distance to set in. This is not what we hoped for, but it becomes unwise to share deeply with someone who is not safe, committed, or trustworthy. People in these types of relationships may stay together but they no longer grow together. They operate within a just-manageable distance. They will attempt to prevent the relationship from drifting farther apart so it doesn't totally unravel, but they cannot or will not work at bringing it closer together. This leaves them with a just-manageable distance from each other.

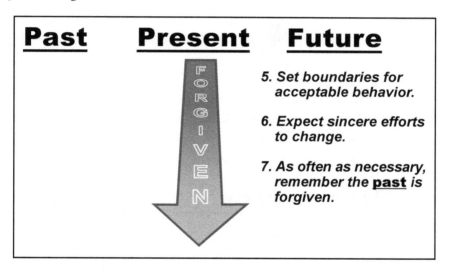

Despite our best efforts to let go of the past and to build healthy relationships in the future, there will be days when the feelings or memories are aroused. When that happens, we need to stop and focus our attention on the Forgiveness Marker we planted that reminds us of the previous work to set us free. We can find great solace in the realization that the fading memory of a past hurtful place or person no longer has the power to pull us down and keep us there. We resolutely choose to stop living in the bondage of the past and recommit our energies to moving forward in building the best "We" relationship possible (step 8).

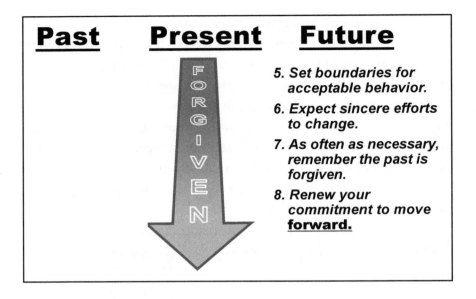

One of the most wonderful promises Jesus offered was, "Come to me, all you who are weary and burdened, and I will give you rest" (Matt. 11:28). Whether it is from the burden of performance or the weariness of unforgiveness, Jesus offers us a much needed rest.

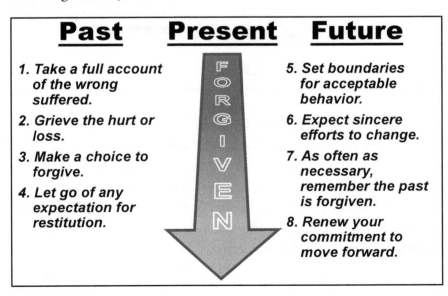

By now, hopefully the people you are helping are beginning to see the benefits of having a strong spiritual foundation for their "We." In addition, you have given them two powerful tools, the Critical Pause and Forgiveness Marker, to help them work through the expected challenges of the "We" workshop. It is rewarding to see their relationships grow stronger. In the next chapter we will discuss how to protect the good work they've done with you in creating a strong "We."

Reflection Questions

1. It is a hard question, but it must be asked. Are there any people in your life, present or past, whom you have not forgiven? Or perhaps tried to forgive, but started at step 3 instead of step 1?

2. Several examples of how to grieve were mentioned. What are some exercises you have found helpful or would like to develop to embrace and release the accumulated hurts?

3. How hard is it for you to let go of any expectation for restitution?

4. What are some of the signs you look for to determine if someone is safe for future relationship?

Chapter 11

TEMPTATION IS MOST EFFECTIVE ON THE NAÏVE AND THE ARROGANT

Station 3 Continued

Having built a strong "We" relationship, you need to carefully guard that work. This would seem to require wisdom, and we all know who the wisest man ever to live was: Solomon. In a tragic irony, however, the wisest man who ever lived gradually fell under the seductive influence of temporal pleasure. Why didn't he see it coming? Why didn't he recognize the warning signs as he began his downward slide? Solomon even wrote a masterful description of the way temptation works and how to avoid it (Proverbs 7). With all his insight into the ways of God and man and all the success this brought him, Solomon failed to employ his best defense: a recognition of his own frailty and a total obedience to the ways of God he knew so well. Let's take a look at what Solomon knew. Later we will explore why he failed to apply it.

In Proverbs 7, Solomon personifies temptation in the form of an adulteress, vividly describing the progressive nature of her seduction. Her target is a naïve young man described in verses 7-9. While the temptation Solomon describes is sexual, the lessons learned from this depiction apply to all forms of temptation. In all its forms, temptation calls us to betray something or someone. We are most at risk to heed its often subtle call when we've foolishly believed we're immune.

Having set the scene, Solomon carefully describes the characteristics and methods of the temptress in verses 10-21. Starting with these verses, Solomon portrays her **personality** as cunning of heart, boisterous, defiant, on the prowl, and lurking at every corner. She knows how to call attention to herself and to what she is offering, and in doing so, she is able to plant images or thoughts in the mind of the young man, giving herself room to maneuver. The advertising and entertainment industries have studied the personality of the adulteress and have become proficient in copying it.

Her **pursuit** (vv. 13-15) is focused and deliberate. The adulteress takes hold of her prey and kisses him. She persuades him with the fortuitous timing of their meeting, suggesting there must be something magical about it. The young man is made to feel special. "I looked for you and have found you!" (v. 15b). I'm reminded of what one husband said to me as he prepared to leave his wife and children for another woman: "Being with my wife is hard work with little return. Being with the other woman requires no work and makes me feel great. How could this be a bad thing?"

One of the core elements of all temptation is the promise of **pleasure** (see vv. 16-18). If the young man is having any second thoughts about going forward with her offer, she fills his imagination with a picture of what is available in her love nest as they drink of love until morning.

Solomon wisely includes a characteristic common to all temptation. It is the classic promise of **protection** (see vv. 19-20). *We won't get caught because my husband is on a long journey. There will be no consequences.* As you watch this scenario unfold, don't you just want to run in, grab this guy, and whisk him away? Lingering on the edge of temptation is like seeing how close you can hold your hand to the flame without getting burned. As he flirts with danger, her **persuasion** (see v. 21) wears him down and finally overpowers whatever slight resistance remained.

The lure builds to a crescendo and reaches a moment of decision. By not running away at this point, the young man's **plight** is sealed (vv. 22-27). Suddenly, his final opportunity to escape is gone. Like an animal that is caught and led to slaughter, his life is lost. What was promised to him as the road to pleasure becomes instead a highway to the grave.

Certain factors caused the young man in Proverbs 7 to be at risk for temptation. He is described as being simple or naïve (see v. 7). He chose to be at the wrong place at the wrong time and was therefore exposed (see v. 8-9). Contrast the characteristics of the young man with the description of the temptress. Who is going to win that match-up?

By not taking his sister (wisdom) and his kinsman (understanding) with him, the young man misses the danger signs (see v. 4). When we are not governed by wisdom and understanding, something else will fill the vacuum. But what does it mean to be controlled by wisdom and understanding? Solomon's instructions (see Prov. 7: 1-3) were to take the commands you know to be true and store them within you, guard them as the apple of your eye, bind them on your fingers, and write them on the tablets of your heart. Our innermost parts must be frequently saturated and sealed with the truth of God's Word (Station 1). Since the young man's heart was not sealed with truth, he was enticed by the flattery of being pursued. Human nature gravitates toward being controlled by something. We all are naïve if we fail to recognize the intensity of the battle that is raging for control of our hearts and minds!

The naïve definitely are at risk, but what about the arrogant? We began the chapter by considering how the wisest man who ever lived, who so insightfully wrote about temptation, could be seduced by temporal pleasure. During my thirty-plus years of working with couples, I have listened to many men and women from all walks of life and Christian service recount their moral failures. I have yet to hear one of them say, "I knew I was at risk." Call it pride, arrogance, or an air of superiority; whatever name you give it, a false notion of invincibility has a way of lowering one's necessary defenses.

Early in my marriage I was fortunate to have a group of godly men to observe. One day I was having lunch with one of the men I considered a model husband and father. I was stunned when he asked me to pray that he would remain faithful to his wife. I didn't know what to say, except to agree to pray. My respect for the man remained high, although there was a nagging sense that I must be missing something. A few years later God gave me the grace to understand the prayer request. His request was not the result of a near failure; it came from an open and honest recognition of his vulnerability. My role model had the godly wisdom to understand that the best weapon against temptation was an honest appraisal of his vulnerability.

When you think of people in the Bible who faced temptation, who comes to mind? Perhaps a better question to ask is, can you think of any characters in the Bible who did not face temptation? I've identified five people who make excellent case studies. Take a few minutes to acquaint yourself with their stories – Eve (Genesis 3:1-6); David (2 Samuel 11); Ananias and Sapphira (Acts 4:32-5:11); and Judas (John 12:4-6 and Matthew 26:14-16).

Although they lived in different eras and faced different types of temptation, there are some commonalities in their stories. To begin with, they all had a desire to **possess** something that was not theirs.

> Eve wanted to possess the **power** of God through knowledge, so she ate the fruit.
> David wanted to possess another **person**, so he summoned Bathsheba.
> Ananias and Sapphira wanted to possess the **prestige** of being important like Barnabas, so they falsified the amount of their offering.
> Judas wanted to possess the financial **perks** of being with Jesus, without entering into a personal relationship with Him, so he pilfered the funds and gained access to the religious leaders.

Likewise, the young man in Proverbs 7 wanted to possess the pleasure offered by another man's wife. And the author of his story, Solomon, wanted to possess the pleasures of foreign wives, including their false gods. It seems that human nature has an insatiable desire to possess what it does not have.

Consider the damage being done today by forces trying to possess power, people, prestige, and the financial perks of being associated with Jesus. What would Jesus say, for example, about Christian symbols being used as advertising strategies to gain personal wealth?

Economic indicators reveal a continuing trend of fewer people possessing a majority of the resources. How much is enough? You might answer this question differently after traveling to some of the most impoverished areas of our cities and rural America or taking a short-term missions trip to one of the many underdeveloped regions of the world. People who return from such ventures often are overwhelmed by the imbalance of resources. I believe one of the greatest indictments on the American evangelical church today is the failure to distribute its wealth to the rest of the body of Christ. We continue to have a desire to possess what is not, and never will be ours!

Our desire to possess has a direct effect on our "We" relationships. An attitude of consumption doesn't just influence our approach to objects. It infiltrates our attitude about what we should be getting from our relationships as well. In other words, the benefits of a relationship, committed or casual, can become just another venue for our consumption. Viewing marriage as a way to possess the benefits of what a spouse has to offer, instead of desiring what is best for that spouse, is a formula for relational disaster.

The drive to possess what is not ours is further fueled by the failure to '**preciate** what God has provided for us. (I am spelling "appreciate" this way in order to maintain the alliteration. The correct way to say it is "perr-she-ate.") A failure to appreciate what they already possessed affected each of our five case studies.

➢ Eve was in **paradise**, but wanted more.
➢ David was in the **palace** with concubines at his disposal, but wanted more.

- ➢ Ananias and Sapphira were in the **peak** experience of the New Testament church, but that wasn't enough.
- ➢ Judas was living in the **presence** of the Son of God, but wanted more.

How could paradise, a palace, a peak experience and even the presence of Jesus fail to produce contentment? It's simple: lack of gratitude. The antidote for the temptation to try to possess what I don't have is gratitude for what I do have.

 Pause to Consider

Two helpful exercises:

If a couple is serious about guarding their relationship against temptation, encourage them to have periodic check-ins that begin by asking each other, "Are there any activities or relationships in my life that you think are putting me at risk?" Their response to this assignment gives you, the helper, three important pieces of information: 1) their comfort level in having such a personal conversation; 2) their receptiveness to feedback; and 3) their willingness to explore the deepest areas of their hearts and minds that may still be under the influence of an old sin nature. The information you receive can be plugged into the following equation:

The amount of hesitancy + the quantity of hidden material = the degree of risk for stumbling into temptation.

Another helpful exercise that drives home the importance of living with gratitude is to have couples imagine God providing them with a transcript of their prayers for the past six months. How much of the transcript would contain expressions of gratitude for the gift of each other?

TEMPTATION IS MOST EFFECTIVE ON THE NAÏVE AND THE ARROGANT

There is always a way to find gratitude. For example, are you grateful for the spouse God chose for you? If you're not sure God chose this spouse, then you can be grateful for the freedom he gave you to choose. If you're concerned that maybe you made a bad choice, then you can be grateful that he is the redeemer of all mistakes. If you don't feel like you have it in you to keep working at a frustrating relationship, then you can be grateful that God will give you a sustaining grace while you receive his provision. If you are unwilling to receive his provision, then you can be grateful that he has shown you that the problem is not your spouse but the condition of your heart. When your heart is cold and resistant, you can be grateful that, "The LORD your God is with you, the Mighty Warrior who saves. He will take great delight in you; in his love he will no longer rebuke you, but will rejoice over you with singing" (Zeph. 3:17). If the God who made this incredible promise seems nonexistent, or at best very distant, you can be grateful that he desires to show himself through the love of your spouse.

It may seem too simplistic to suggest that gratitude and temptation are a matter of focus. If you were asked to make a list of your friend's or spouse's strengths and weaknesses, which column would be longer? The more you focus on the weaknesses, the greater the risk that you will justify whatever it is that temptation is promising you. The more focus you place on the strengths, the greater your potential for becoming grateful. I'm not suggesting that weaknesses should go unattended. I am suggesting they not be given a disproportionate amount of focus. It is impossible to experience contempt and gratitude at the same time. Which one will fill your heart?

"Let the peace of Christ rule in your hearts, since as members of one body you were called to peace. And *be thankful*. Let the word of Christ dwell in you richly as you teach and admonish one another with all wisdom through psalms, hymns and songs from the Spirit, singing to God with *gratitude in your hearts*. And whatever you do, whether in word or deed, do it all in the name of the Lord Jesus, *giving thanks* to God the Father through him" (Col. 3:15-17, emphasis added).

143

Here is a sobering final thought: Our attempts to possess God's provision for personal gain will always lead to death—if not physical, as in the case of our examples, then certainly spiritual.

Paul made sure his young apprentice, Timothy, understood how quickly his effectiveness as a spiritual leader would be diminished if he didn't comprehend the principles of possession and gratitude (see 1 Tim. 6:3-10). At the conclusion of his first letter to Timothy, Paul wrote these words, "But godliness with contentment is great gain" (1 Tim. 6:6). Paul's lesson for Timothy and for us was to choose a life of gratitude and a desire to possess only that which God designed for us to enjoy with his fullest blessing.

As you prepare to move into Station 4, it may be helpful to review the flow of the first three stations. All the transformational work taking place in these stations cannot be contained. If we try to stop the flow at Station 3, we will have missed our kingdom purpose. Our closest relationships, including marriage, were never designed to be an end, but a means to make a difference in the lives of others. Unfortunately, there is a significant amount of misguided Christian teaching that makes having a great marriage the ultimate goal. A great marriage, however you define it, was never intended by God to be the goal. The greatest fulfillment and joy in our "We" relationships is actually a by-product of proper alignment with God's kingdom purposes as carried out in Station 4.

Reflection Questions

1. What lessons can be learned about temptation from the temptress and the vulnerability of the naïve young man from the Proverbs 7 illustration?

   Here are a few examples of today's equivalent to Proverbs 7 that may help in your reflection of risk factors. Are you:

_____ Viewing late night television or becoming involved in online activities after your spouse has gone to bed?

_____ Spending time away from home for business or ministry with no accountability?

_____ Enjoying conversations with a work partner that shift from professional to flirtatious?

_____ Building a new or resuming an old romantic relationship through social media that is unknown to your spouse?

_____ Failing to establish an accountability partner in your life, other than your spouse, who knows when you are struggling, even if you try to deny it?

2. My mentor understood that recognizing his vulnerability was his best defense. Where are you at risk for underestimating your vulnerability?

3. What are you trying to possess that is not yours? If you are not sure, ask the Holy Spirit to convict your heart.

4. Where do you need to make a shift in your attitude toward gratitude?

Chapter 12

OUR KINGDOM PURPOSE

Station 4

By the time Ted reached his mid-sixties, most of his life goals were met. He envisioned this season of life as a time to enjoy the benefits of his hard work. Instead, he experienced an unsettledness that simmered just below the surface. Ted soon realized that his restless sleep, trouble concentrating, and loss of energy were important warning signs. We began a dialogue to explore what they were telling him.

Ted thought his symptoms were related to a lack of exercise, so he and his wife Cathy began taking long walks together. I asked him what they talked about on their walks. He thought for a minute and said, "Most of our conversations are about how much we dislike the aging process." He continued, "Lately, it seems we've been doing quite a bit of reminiscing." When Ted mentioned the reminiscing, his countenance changed. Ted and Cathy, like many others their age, were taking an inventory of what their lives had been about. There were many positive highlights from their family vacations, special holidays, and the joys of raising three active boys, but Ted's troubled look meant something else was going on. He said, "I can't really explain it, but when I look back on my life it seems like something is missing."

Over the next several weeks, Ted continued to put words to what was going on inside. As his story took shape, the missing piece came into focus. By all of today's standards, Ted was a great husband and father. He wasn't perfect, but he had provided well for his family's financial, emotional, and relational needs. His regret was not about how he cared for his family but about how he had allowed his family's well-being to become his ultimate goal instead of a means to fulfill a much larger kingdom purpose.

God never intended for Ted, or any of us, to hoard his love and to keep all the benefits of our personal and relational growth to ourselves. The kingdom that Jesus came to establish, as highlighted by Station 4, requires us to use the overflow of the gifts and lessons learned in Stations 1 – 3 to reach out to those who have not heard about God's love or had it shown to them. Ted's regret was that he had prevented Cathy and his children from experiencing the deepest joy of using their gifts to benefit others. Ted also felt remorse that his family's inward focus had deprived others of experiencing God's love through them.

Thankfully, as we've already seen, there are no wasted experiences in God's redemptive plan. Ted confessed his self-centeredness and short-sightedness. He then joined with Cathy in a season of prayer to make God's kingdom and his righteousness their first priority (see Matt. 6:33). The joy of proper alignment with God's design made all their other relationships even richer.

In a similar way, Paul invited the Corinthian believers to conduct a review of their lives and to see if they were investing their best energies toward things of lasting value in the kingdom. Using a construction metaphor, he began by addressing the foundation on which the Corinthian Christians were building (1 Cor. 3:10-11). Any foundation other than Jesus Christ would not last.

Next, Paul focused on the construction of the building. He listed the building materials commonly used in their day ranging from the most expensive to the least: "gold, silver, costly stones, wood, hay, or straw" (v. 12).

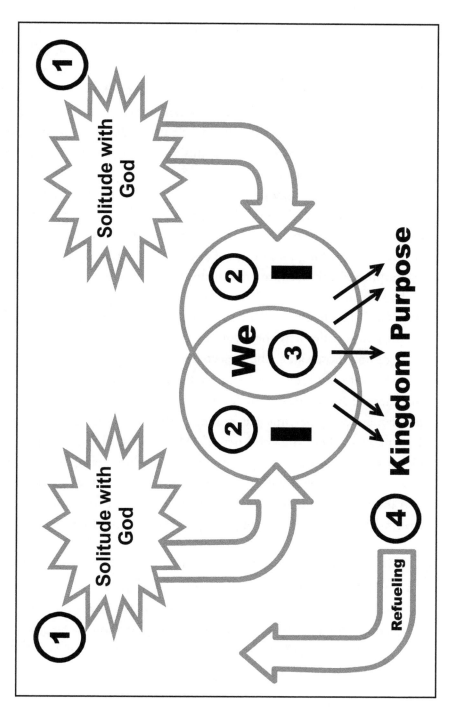

Paul continued with a warning that all work will be scrutinized on "the Day," referring to Christ's return, when the judgment fire will reveal the quality of each person's work (v. 13). Life work done according to God's Word and under the influence of the Holy Spirit will pass the test and a reward will be given. Life investments not built according to God's purposes will be consumed by this fire and lost. Paul concluded by saying that the person who lives this way "will be saved, but only as one escaping through the flames" (v. 15).

In essence Paul is saying that there are some who received Christ as their Savior and asked him to be their foundation, which gained them entrance into heaven. Then for some reason they decided not to live according to his kingdom's ways of operating, and consequently, all they accomplished and accumulated in this world had no eternal value and will be consumed by fire. The good news is that they will spend eternity with God. The bad news is that they enter eternity empty-handed. We might well wonder why they would want to spend an eternity living in a kingdom whose values they rejected while living on earth.

So what does kingdom living look like? We started our discussion in chapter 1 by recalling how Jesus started his public ministry with the proclamation: "The time has come ... the kingdom of God is near. Repent and believe the good news!" (Mark 1:15). He then went on to give his first followers clear guidelines for kingdom living. In those first few weeks Jesus spent with his eager yet uncertain followers, he taught and modeled for them what it meant to live in the kingdom of God, from which we can glean five principles for our kingdom life.

1. **We will have a new focus in our work**. It is called having a "kingdom purpose."

   As Jesus walked beside the Sea of Galilee, he saw Simon and his brother Andrew casting a net into the lake, for they were fishermen. "Come, follow me," Jesus said, "and I will send you out to fish for people." At once they left their nets and followed him (Mark 1:16-18).

Jesus made it clear in his invitation to Simon and Andrew that if they were going to follow him the focus of their work would change from being fishermen to becoming fishers of men. Having a kingdom purpose required Simon and Andrew to shift their focus and energies from making a living to showing people how to find true life in Christ. For some individuals you're helping, the call to become a fisher of men may require a change in their employment. A change of this magnitude often prompts a variety of responses from others, not all of which are positive. That should not be surprising; in fact, it can be expected because living with a kingdom purpose means seeing things that others cannot.

For others, becoming a fisher of men does not require a change in what they do, but a shift in how they do it, who they influence while doing it, under whose power it is done, and who receives glory for it. These four criteria provide a good springboard for discussion with the people you are helping as they evaluate whether their current approach to work, ministry, relationships, or studies has kingdom significance.

As Ted reviewed how well his life work reflected a kingdom purpose, he was generally encouraged by his positive responses to the needs that had been presented to him. Unfortunately, because of his exclusive focus on doing what was best for his family, he had become increasingly insulated from the needs of those outside his immediate community. Ted had what I describe as a "passive generosity." He responded kindly when someone made him aware of the needs of those who were hurting, but because his world had become so insulated, people with needs had no way of gaining access to his generosity. With regret, he confessed his lack of intentionality about acting on what he believed.

2. **We will have a new source of power**. In the kingdom, we receive an invitation to "walk in the Spirit."

   They went to Capernaum, and when the Sabbath came, Jesus went into the synagogue and began to teach. The people were amazed at his teaching, because he taught them as one who had <u>authority</u>, not as the teachers of the law. Just then a man in their synagogue who was possessed by an impure *spirit cried out, "What do you want with us, Jesus of Nazareth? Have you come to destroy us? I know who you are—the Holy One of God!" "Be quiet!" said Jesus sternly. "Come out of him!" The impure spirit shook the man violently and came out of him with a shriek. The people were all so amazed that they asked each other, "What is this? A new teaching—and with <u>authority</u>! He even gives orders to impure spirits and they obey him." News about him spread quickly over the whole region of Galilee* (Mark 1:21-28, emphasis added).

It is not possible to accomplish kingdom tasks on our strength. When we enter a kingdom that operates in a spiritual realm, we must operate under the full influence of the Holy Spirit. The apostle Paul understood this source of power when he wrote, "I came to you in weakness with great fear and trembling. My message and my preaching were not with wise and persuasive words, but with a demonstration of the Spirit's power, so that your faith might not rest on human wisdom, but on God's power" (1 Cor. 2:3-5).

Just before he ascended to heaven, Jesus commanded his followers to go to Jerusalem and wait until they received the gift of the Holy Spirit and were clothed with power from God (Acts 1:4 & 8). Even though they had already experienced the power of the Holy Spirit miraculously working through them on the two occasions when Jesus sent them out (Luke 9 & 10), they were still not properly equipped for the work ahead. What was missing?

From their first encounter with the authority of Jesus' words and works until their time of waiting in Jerusalem, the disciples were gradually catching on that Jesus wanted to share with them the same power source he enjoyed, the Spirit in him. Jesus knew this transfer of power required that he depart from them so he could send his Spirit back to live within them (John 16:7). Jesus was so confident in what the transfer of power would do for the disciples that he made this incredible statement: "Very truly I tell you, whoever believes in me will do the works I have been doing, and they will do even greater things than these, because I am going to the Father" (John 14:12). The disciples had tasted the power of the Holy Spirit, now they would have him living in them.

How do we know if the help we offer is coming from our strength or is from the Holy Spirit? Maybe, like the disciples, we've tasted the moving of the Spirit but haven't yet learned how to live with his presence as the source of power for everything we do. If this is the case, then perhaps, as was the case with the disciples, we are not yet prepared to do what will be required. I am certain that even the best human efforts or skill cannot set people free from the grip of sin or heal them from its devastating effects. Proper training is imperative and skill development essential, but they are only effective when they are being directed by the power of the Holy Spirit. If this is uncertain territory for you as a helper, perhaps Jesus is inviting you to go to your place of waiting and stay there until you've learned what it means to be clothed with the power of the Holy Spirit.

It is important to note that those who were waiting in Jerusalem for the fulfillment of Jesus' promise "all joined together constantly in prayer" (Acts 1:14). Jesus' followers knew the importance of taking time to step aside from the demands of busy schedules in order to be still and listen because he modeled this behavior for them starting with the early days of his ministry.

3. **We will have a new starting point**. It requires solitude.

> *That evening after sunset the people brought to Jesus all the sick and demon-possessed. The whole town gathered at the door, and Jesus healed many who had various diseases. He also drove out many demons, but he would not let the demons speak because they knew who he was. Very early in the morning, while it was still dark, Jesus got up, left the house and went off to a solitary place, where he prayed. Simon and his companions went to look for him, and when they found him, they exclaimed: "Everyone is looking for you!" Jesus replied, "Let us go somewhere else—to the nearby villages—so I can preach there also. That is why I have come" (Mark 1:32-38).*

After an unforgettable evening of healing and deliverance, the disciples woke up the next morning ready to pick up where things left off.

You can imagine their excitement at the possibilities of what they assumed was about to happen. The power unleashed by Jesus the night before was exactly what was needed to unify a nation and to re-establish Israel to her place of prominence. A crowd was gathering and the atmosphere was electric, but where was Jesus? He had gone out to a solitary place to be still and pray in order to remain focused on the kingdom of God.

Jesus must have been exhausted by the events that took place the day before in the synagogue and at the home of Simon and Andrew. Yet he knew that the empowerment he received from time alone with the Father was much more valuable than anything extra sleep could give him. In addition to using this time for spiritual refreshment, I wonder if Jesus was also fighting the desire to stay and care for the people he loved instead of moving on to the next town to preach the good news there. The abruptness of his departure suggests that he may have been feeling the strain of being pulled in two different directions. Whatever Jesus talked about with the Father during this solitary time gave him the power and perspective for what to do next.

Every helper who desires to operate according to kingdom-of-God principles must learn from Jesus' example of what it means to have a daily rhythm of inflow and outflow. How much energy can helpers expend in the outflow of Stations 3 and 4 without taking time to refuel with the inflow from Stations 1 and 2?

Allowing ourselves to become depleted, according to Paul, is a formula that makes us susceptible to the influences of the world we are working against (see Eph. 5). His advice for preventing this is to experience an ongoing filling with the Holy Spirit (see v. 18). When Paul equates being filled with the Spirit to being drunk with wine, he seems to understand that human nature wants to be influenced. If we are not being influenced by what comes out of our times of solitude and stillness, the clarity of our kingdom work suffers, the life-changing movements of the Spirit are replaced with our feeble efforts, and although we may avoid being drunk with wine, we become addicted to the "high" of doing good and being recognized for it.

Living in a world that is increasingly anti-solitude means we have our work cut out for us. It seems that there is an all-out campaign to make sure we never have to be alone with our thoughts. Some of your best help in guiding people toward kingdom living will be to conduct an intervention that cuts them off their addiction to information updates, videos of how other people live, or superficial contacts with people who don't care to know them. We give them life-changing patterns when we help them develop the disciplines of noticing, reflecting, and listening during their times of solitude. These disciplines position us well for our next step in kingdom living.

4. **We will have a new heart toward others.** It is characterized by compassion.

A man with leprosy came to him and begged him on his knees, "If you are willing, you can make me clean." Jesus was indignant. He reached out and touched the man. "I am willing," he said. "Be clean!" Immediately the leprosy left him and he was cleansed (Mark 1:40-42).

As the disciples moved about with Jesus and listened to his teachings, they were becoming more familiar with him and his message. Just when they started to relax, Jesus was confronted by a leper. As the leper fell to his knees and begged Jesus to make him clean, I wonder what the disciples were thinking about this man who had just broken the law by entering into close proximity to them.

Jesus, filled with compassion, reached out his hand and touched the man. "I am willing, be clean." As if the healing itself weren't enough, Jesus chose to administer it through a compassionate touch. I wonder when the leper had last been touched. I wonder if the disciples were more focused on the fact that Jesus just broke the ceremonial law than that he extended a compassionate, healing touch. What did the disciples learn about kingdom living from witnessing the deep compassion Jesus had for someone on the extreme margin of society? Similarly, what can we as helpers learn about how Jesus may want to use us to reach out to those who are marginalized?

There is a difference between doing loving things, and truly loving someone. We should be cautious to avoid judging people's motives, but doing loving things may be more about how it makes me feel in contrast to truly loving someone whatever the cost or inconvenience. I am not discounting the benefit of doing kind things for others. I am, however, suggesting that there are times when true compassion is shown by loving one's enemies, praying for those who mistreat you (see Matt. 5:44), giving anonymously (see Matt. 6:3-4), and loving those who make others feel uncomfortable (see Matt. 5:46-48).

Pause to Consider

What is the difference between what Jesus saw when he looked at people and what we see? When the pleading leper knelt before him with his request, who did Jesus see? When he spoke to or hung out with the prostitutes, addicts, and tax-collecting thieves, what did Jesus see in them? I believe Jesus saw sin-disfigured bodies and souls becoming clean and made whole though the blood of his life-changing sacrifice.

His potential for cleansing becomes the great equalizer in how we view people! The most flagrant sinner and the most religiously pious person are seen as the same. If we take away the categories that a sin-infected world uses to judge people's worth, we catch a glimpse of what Jesus saw—a unique person created in the image of God to be loved and enjoyed. Seeing people through Jesus' eyes removes the prejudicial categories of race, gender, culture, and degrees of sinfulness. With the gift of his vision, we too can respond with a warm embrace and words of life-giving hope to all we encounter.

Perhaps some people are just naturally more compassionate than others, but I have to wonder where that kind of compassion comes from. Beginning counselors are taught the importance of feeling empathy toward their clients. Jesus seems to be describing an empathy that is on steroids! How do we go beyond feeling sorry for the misfortunate to embracing them with all the compassion Jesus expressed to the leper?

Since kingdom living means seeing people as God sees them, who in your life needs to be seen as God sees them? Who is saying to you, "If you are willing I need your help, love, attention, encouragement, and time"?

5. **We will have a new way of doing relationships.** In this new way, relationships are "God's workshop."

> *As he walked along, he saw Levi son of Alphaeus sitting at the tax collector's booth. "Follow me," Jesus told him, and Levi got up and followed him* (Mark 2:14).

In order to grasp the significance of Jesus' invitation to Levi (also called Matthew) the tax collector, we need to understand that Levi was an opportunist who aligned himself with Rome in order to profit from his countrymen. He had no scruples. He stole from those who had very little. Levi was the polar opposite of everything we have just learned about compassion. Tax collectors were so despised, they were excommunicated from the life of the community.

Can you imagine the introductions when Jesus invited Levi to join his inner circle? "Simon the zealot—dedicated to fighting against Rome and anything it represents, meet Levi the tax collector, a Roman sympathizer. Now that you've met, I expect you to get to know each other and work well together." What was Jesus thinking trying to bring these two characters together? To say the least, this added an interesting twist to the group dynamic.

A kingdom way of living views relationships as God's workshop. How the disciples learned to resolve the conflicts generated by their various beliefs and strong personalities was an important part of the training. What they learned about themselves during this process would have great value in their gradual movement toward becoming like Christ.

These were hard lessons for proud men to learn. Their rivalries continued until the final days before Jesus' crucifixion. In one last powerful teaching about humility and serving one another, Jesus washed the disciples' feet the night before he died for them.

In a fallen world, conflict is an inevitable part of relationships. From a kingdom point of view, the resolution of conflicts helps us achieve trust and relational depth. It is hard to trust someone until we see how they treat us when we disagree. When we go to the hard places relationally and learn to work through our differences, a God-honoring unity is produced. This display of unity provides the credibility to speak into the lives of others embroiled in personal and institutional conflict.

Jesus' invitation to Levi rescued him from his life of corruption. It must have been hard for Levi to break into the inner circle of Jesus' companions. Have you ever wondered why Jesus didn't put the professional accountant, Levi, in charge of the group's finances? This was Judas' job and he took full advantage of it by skimming off the top (see John 12:4-6). I see Levi pulling Judas off to the side and saying, "As a former professional thief, I know what you're doing." How must the repentant Levi have felt about Jesus relying on Judas, the unrepentant thief, to do what he was best equipped to do? This was an area where Levi could have contributed and made himself important to the group, but Jesus chose to withhold this opportunity from him.

Levi didn't know it at the time, but Jesus had a much more significant role for him to play. A kingdom way of operating sees God's redemptive power in taking a sinner like Levi and using his skills for things that have eternal significance. According to Whyte in his book *Bible Characters of The New Testament,* Levi was a detail man who would provide the most thorough recording of Jesus' teachings, the Gospel of Matthew.

Whether we like it or not, relationships are God's workshop. I can choose to protest my lab partners, or choose to let conflict be the teacher that prepares me for kingdom service.

How closely are you following the kingdom living template that Jesus gave his disciples? Perhaps you are at a point of transition much like Ted and Cathy and need to step back and do a life review. If that is where you find yourself, the following review questions would be a useful place to start.

**Life Review Questions based on Jesus'
Model for Kingdom Living**

1. What is the ultimate purpose of your work? Are you making a living (a fisherman) or teaching people how to live (becoming fishers of men)?

2. What is your source of power? How much of what you do each day is attempted on your strength, and how much is the result of a daily infusion of the Holy Spirit's power?

3. How committed are you to developing regular patterns of solitude as the starting point for gaining and maintaining a kingdom-of-God focus? How are the disciplines of noticing, listening, and reflecting being incorporated into your tasks and relationships?

4. Are you driven more by duty or compassion? Who is saying to you, "If you are willing, you could really make a difference in my life?"

5. If relationships are God's workshop, what lessons are you currently learning as you interact with the people in your life? Ask several people who know you well the following questions: "Do I come across as being open to feedback?" "Do you see me as someone who is willing to learn from others?"

As you sort through these questions with the people you're helping, be sure to point out how they are now consolidating the lessons learned from the previous three stations. It is encouraging to realize how the concepts they've been exploring are fitting together to create a new way of being.

The final chapter continues to build on Jesus' model for how to love and serve individuals in Station 4. There I will tell you about a ten-year-old boy who taught me how to do good therapy.

Reflection Questions:

1. Ted described his lack of intentionality in helping those who were hurting as a "passive generosity." Where has God been prompting you to be more intentional about providing some form of help to others?

2. As you reflect on your answers to the life review questions, what are some specific next steps for you to take? Who are the people you've chosen to help you make progress?

Alexander Whyte, *Bible Characters: The New Testament* (C. Tinling & Co., 1958), 49.

Chapter 13

A Few Final Thoughts

Station 4 Continued

If there were a hall of fame for caseworkers, the vote for Pam's induction would be unanimous. She was a tireless advocate for the voiceless victims of abuse. As a psychology intern, I viewed a referral from her with mixed emotions. I needed to see as many clients as possible to accumulate hours, but as a beginning therapist I felt woefully inadequate to handle the complex cases she sent me. This one would be my most challenging.

My first meeting with Jack went as well as can be expected when an adult is trying to find common ground with a ten-year-old. He was not happy to be there, but we managed to make the best of it. The turning point in our interaction came when I began talking with him about baseball. With a little bit of research I found out that Jack's passion in life was playing on his Little League baseball team. We talked about his favorite professional players and how his team was doing. For our next several sessions I received permission from his mother and my supervisor to play catch with Jack as we talked. After a month of weekly visits we had played lots of catch, but Jack had clearly decided that baseball was the only acceptable topic for conversation. Each attempt to probe into his personal life was stonewalled by a redirect back to baseball or met with silence.

I was having doubts about my ability to get Jack to open up. Although Jack wasn't talking to me, he had been communicating through his disruptive behavior at school and home that his world was falling apart. A previously well-behaved, bright student, he was getting into fights on the playground and failing several subjects. The last straw that prompted his mother to seek professional help was the hole he punched through the drywall in his bedroom.

Jack's choice to express his frustrations through violence was modeled for him by a dad who was a mean drunk. Until recently Jack's mom had been the only target of his dad's outbursts. As the violence progressed from shouting to shoving and then to punching, Jack tried to come to his mother's defense. His bravery provided a temporary reprieve for his mother but caused the violence to be redirected toward him.

Watching her oldest son get slapped around provided the jolt needed for Jack's mom to take action. Social Services sprang into action and his dad was removed from the house, but the damage had been done.

Jack's fear of living with an unpredictable alcoholic father was replaced with the frustration of having to care for his two younger siblings while his mother tried to make ends meet. The extra home responsibilities meant very little time for baseball. The adult-sized responsibilities overwhelmed the emotional reserves of this ten-year-old. His cry for help was expressed with a fist through the wall. Help was now available, but Jack wondered if it could be trusted.

Fortunately for me and for Jack, I had an experienced supervisor who suggested I give our time of playing catch a few more weeks. The caseworker agreed and also informed me that Jack's dad was out on parole and had been granted a supervised visit with him. This would be Jack's first contact with his dad since his dad's removal from the house.

After about ten minutes of catch that week I asked Jack what he and his dad would do during their visit. I noticed that the ball came back to me with a bit more zip. After a few minutes of silence, I asked if his dad would also be visiting with his younger brothers. Jack's throw came back with an uncharacteristic wildness. He was beginning to crack. The question that opened the floodgate of tears and powered a fastball that stung my hand was, "What would you like to say to your dad?"

Through a combination of sobs and clenched teeth, Jack blamed his dad, the beer, his mom, the company that laid off his dad, and even himself for the breakup of his family. This cathartic release provided some rich therapeutic material for the conversations that followed over the next several weeks. We still played catch, but now our time included conversations about what was bothering him and what he could do about it. Baseball continued to be a helpful medium for discussing life issues. One of our best conversations about how to manage frustrations came when I asked him, "Has an umpire ever called you 'out' when you were safe?" He replied that it had happened twice. The first time he said he "pitched a fit" and his coach benched him. The second time he gave the umpire a dirty look and ran off the field. I did not need to draw any parallels because Jack had the street smarts to know where I was going and in return he smirked.

Although life still had lots of challenges as his single mom tried to provide a quality life for her kids, Jack was once again thriving in his world of home, school, and baseball. Jack and I agreed that we could now meet every other week as we began to wind down our time together. Because the weather conditions were no longer conducive to playing catch, Jack and I were addressing his life issues while we battled aliens on a computer game. In what was agreed to be his last visit, I was surprised when Jack showed up with his baseball and glove. Was he having a change of mind about ending our sessions? Was he slipping back into some previous patterns? Was the loss of a caring male in his life too difficult to face?

What Jack did next made a lasting impression on me as a person and as a therapist. He taught me a lesson that surpassed anything I had yet learned from a textbook or lecture. Jack walked over to my desk and opened the drawer where I kept my baseball glove. He took his ball and put it in my glove. He looked me in the eyes and spoke these words from a place of deep conviction, "You can use this ball with other guys who need to play catch." His prized possession was being donated for the purpose of helping others.

As a ten-year-old, Jack understood something that eludes many adults. Everything he experienced in his healing process was to be made available to others who were still hurting. This is the crux of Station 4. Although he didn't have the vocabulary to express this powerful biblical truth, he was fulfilling the command to love as we've been loved (see John 15:12).

 Pause to Consider

Jack's incredible gesture of giving his baseball for others exemplifies Jesus' teaching, "…Any of you who does not give up everything he has cannot be my disciple" (Luke 14:33). This amazing ten-year-old taught me a life lesson about making all our possessions and experiences available for kingdom service. Jack reminds us that we have much to learn from the people we help and from the process through which that help is given.

I believe one of the best predictors of longevity and impact as a helper is the ability to be a provider and student at the same time. Even when using clear biblical guidelines to address blatant sinful behaviors, a workman (helper) approved by God handles these truths correctly in their content and context (see 2 Tim. 2:15), and presents them in a spirit of humility and love as a fellow learner.

I pray that we will never see ourselves as spiritual or mental health experts, but as apprentices who carefully observe and emulate the movements of the One who is close to the brokenhearted and saves those who are crushed in spirit (see Ps. 34:18). Consider for a moment the perspective of someone being helped. Do you think this person would rather work with a helper who approaches the relationship as a fellow learner or with a helper who comes across as the expert who tells them what they're doing wrong and how they should fix it? By maintaining the position of fellow learner, we also avoid promising more than can be delivered, and have the freedom to try out new approaches that will increase our effectiveness.

What Jack taught me about helping others

I wish I could say that all, or even most of my counseling experiences were as successful as my time with Jack. The reality is that each meeting contains a mixture of things that go well and not so well. Even seasoned helpers look back on a session and second-guess what they did or realize something they missed. We all hope that each meeting will afford us the opportunity to sharpen our skills and find even better ways of helping others.

I learned five key lessons in my work with Jack that I like to share with other helpers who have that same desire to get better at what we do. Some of the suggestions may already be a part of your repertoire. Hopefully, you will pick up a couple of tips to improve your effectiveness.

1) Start well

As a beginning therapist, I learned that before starting my first session with Jack I needed to do some background research to discover his areas of interest. Collecting this information allowed me to direct our conversation toward Jack's two passions: Little League baseball and computer games. I was quite comfortable asking questions about Little League but needed to brush up on his favorite computer games. My goal was not just to appear knowledgeable, but to use what I knew and had learned about Jack to ask questions that would allow Jack to be the expert in some area of our work together. The awkward imbalance of power between client and helper is redistributed when the helper recognizes the client for what he has to contribute to the conversation. Jack was the expert on Little League baseball and computer games. I was eager to learn what he could teach me. By beginning our conversations with subjects in Jack's comfort zone, we were able to develop a pattern of communication that would gradually permit us to move into the more uncomfortable areas.

2) Recognize the real issue(s)

Jack's mother and teachers were focused on changing his behavior, and rightly so. However, it would have been a mistake for me to try to make these changes before we had established a relationship of trust. As the relationship developed, I began to understand that the surface behaviors were a form of communication. In the only way he knew how, Jack was communicating, "My world is falling apart and I don't know how to make it better." His disruptive behavior, although unacceptable, was merely the symptom of a deeper issue. I chose to temporarily bypass the symptom in order to pursue the underlying cause of his bad behavior.

Many adults who seek help are also interested in getting relief from their symptoms. Be careful you are not helping them find better ways to manage their plugs (chapter 1) as a way to avoid the deeper issues.

3) Trust the process

Either due to our personality or because of a strong desire to see the people we're helping make progress, sometimes it is hard for helpers to be patient with the therapeutic process. I was ready to concede that playing catch was not accomplishing the treatment goals. I shudder to think of what my impatience could have done to make Jack even more distrustful of adult males.

Many helpers can become impatient when they don't see change taking place. My counseling students get tired of hearing me say, "Trust the process." Please do not underestimate the therapeutic value of your focused attention on the person you are helping, even when they seem not to be progressing. Also, remember that the Spirit-guided process can be trusted because of who is in control. You may want to create a reminder for yourself that reads, "A good process will lead to a great product."

4) Draw out

With so much information at our disposal, it is easy to see ourselves as dispensers of informed advice. Helpers who are received well by the people they help resist the urge to put more information into a person's thought process and instead spend more time drawing out what is already there. A well-worded, well-timed question often has significantly more benefit than even some of the best advice we can give. As someone who enjoys teaching, I was surprised when I reflected on my time with Jack and realized that before his cathartic moment, I had given him no advice. Jack had enough people speaking into his life about what he needed to change. Without realizing it, I had become the place where he was accepted. Some of my attempts to draw him out weren't very helpful. Perhaps because he felt accepted, Jack was patient with me as I labored to provide what he needed. When the timing was right, I couldn't have stopped what needed to come out, even if I had tried.

5) Shift from self to others

When the people we're helping begin to live in Station 4, they give less attention to their own concerns and needs. Instead, they begin to focus on how they can use their experiences for the benefit of others. The transformed heart that is filled with love naturally reaches out to those in need. Jack did not know who else would need to play catch, but he was determined to do everything within his power to make sure they would have a ball to use when the time came. It didn't require a lot of thought for Jack and he certainly didn't ask for any recognition. He simply acted out of a natural response of gratitude to do what he could to help others.

Twenty-plus years later, I remain grateful for Jack's example of what living in Station 4 looks like. In chapter 12 we examined what Jesus wanted his disciples to know about kingdom living. The chart below provides a final summary of the model Jesus provided for us to help others. If we claim to be his followers, then it would seem imperative for us to study and replicate his approach in our personal lives and in our communities of faith.

Jesus' Model	Our Tendencies
✓1. Invest energy in presenting the good news of the kingdom and meeting needs. (Matt. 4:23-25; 5)	Invest our energy in keeping the machinery running smoothly, e.g., programs, procedures, and policies.
2. Take a few and go deep. (Luke 8:51; 9:28)	Spread ourselves thin and stay shallow.
3. Pursue the people the world rejects. (Matt. 4:18-25; 9:35-38; Luke 19:5-10; James 2:1-10)	Pursue the people the world values.
4. Engage in fellowship with people who are from different backgrounds and walks of life. (Matt. 9:9-12)	Embrace only those who think and act like us.
5. Meet people where they are. (Matt. 8:28; 9:2; John 4:7)	Tell people who they need to be.
6. Examine the condition of the heart. (Matt. 6:1-5)	Concentrate on outward appearances and behaviors.
7. Discern and join what the Holy Spirit has already initiated. (Acts 8:26)	Set agendas that are under our control and timing.
8. Teach the crowds, but love individuals. (Luke 5:17-26; 7:11-15; 8:40-48; 18:35-43; 19:1-10)	Love the crowds (big numbers at our events), but have trouble finding time for individuals.
9. Call people to repent and follow. (Matt. 4:17-19)	Invite people to be saved and continue living as they did before, only with eternal security.

A Few Final Thoughts

Jesus' Model	Our Tendencies
10. Speak and minister with authority. (Matt. 7:28-29)	Depend on cultural relevance and entertaining delivery systems.
11. Be still and enter into periods of deep communion with the Father. (Ps. 46:10; Luke 4:42; Matt. 14:23)	Become preoccupied with doing what is good (under our strength), but miss what is best (prayerful reliance on the power and timing of the Holy Spirit).

I am grateful that God has given you the desire to help others. I trust you will find him faithful to provide everything you need to make an eternally significant difference in the lives of the people you help.

Reflection Questions

1. What is God asking you to do or to give for the benefit of others?

2. Spend some time reviewing how you get started in your helping relationships. Are there any preparatory steps you could take to help people feel well-received by you (e.g., getting to know their areas of interest or creating opportunities for them to share areas of expertise)?

3. Think of someone you are currently helping or have recently helped. Make a list of their symptoms and then list their potentially deeper issues.

4. What does it mean to you to trust the process?

5. Experiment with some conversations where you are focused exclusively on drawing out more information from another person by asking good follow-up questions.

6. How well are you following Jesus' model for how to help others? Which of your tendencies are in opposition to his model?

Permission is given for the
book purchaser to reproduce the
Appendices.

Larry R. Wagner, Ph.D. 2015

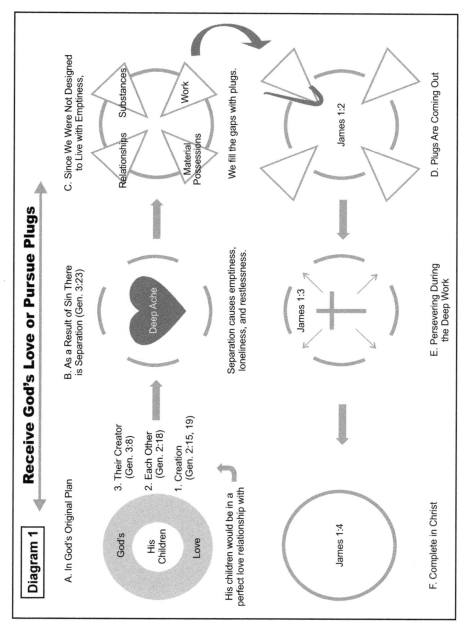

Diagram 1

Receive God's Love or Pursue Plugs

A. In God's Original Plan

God's — His Children — Love

3. Their Creator (Gen. 3:8)
2. Each Other (Gen. 2:18)
1. Creation (Gen. 2:15, 19)

His children would be in a perfect love relationship with

B. As a Result of Sin There is Separation (Gen. 3:23)

Deep Ache

Separation causes emptiness, loneliness, and restlessness.

C. Since We Were Not Designed to Live with Emptiness,

Substances
Work
Relationships
Material Possessions

We fill the gaps with plugs.

D. Plugs Are Coming Out

James 1:2

James 1:3

James 1:4

E. Persevering During the Deep Work

F. Complete in Christ

173

Appendix B: The Four Stations

Larry R. Wagner, Ph.D. 2015

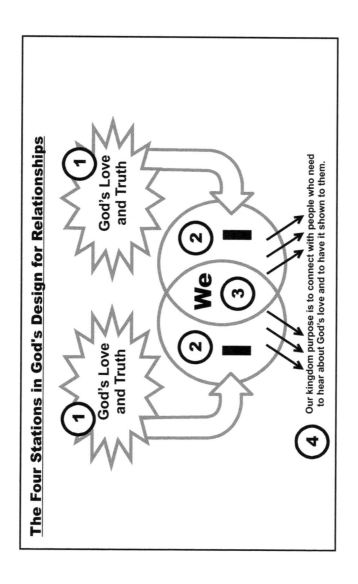

The Four Stations in God's Design for Relationships

1 God's Love and Truth

1 God's Love and Truth

2 — We 3 2 —

4 Our kingdom purpose is to connect with people who need to hear about God's love and to have it shown to them.

Appendix C: The Inner Room

Larry R. Wagner, Ph.D. 2015

My Inner Room

I. What sends me there:
- Painful memories from the past
- Not being appreciated or treated the way I think I should be
- Rejection / criticism
- Frustration in my important relationships
- Comparisons to others who seem to have everything going for them

II. When I go to my Inner Room, I often feel:
- ➤ Guilty
- ➤ Lonely
- ➤ Unfairly treated
- ➤ Insecure
- ➤ Like giving up
- ➤ Disappointed with myself or others
- ➤ Angry

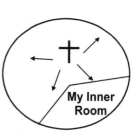

III. What I do there:
- ✓ Fill up on sadness
- ✓ Replay the hurts
- ✓ Get frustrated with what is wrong with me, my family, my friends, my school, etc
- ✓ Remind myself that others can't be trusted
- ✓ Fantasize about escapes such as becoming extremely successful so others will recognize how incredible I really am
- ✓ Wait until I can find someone to rescue me
- ✓ Find ways of manipulating people into meeting my needs

IV. Types of responses that come from this toxic fuel:

- ❖ Make plans to stay very busy (anesthesia of busyness) so that I don't have to deal with things
- ❖ Don't get too close to anyone who could see the real me
- ❖ Get angry with the people who have not treated me well
- ❖ Think about how much better life would be if only ...
- ❖ Criticize others in order to keep the focus away from me
- ❖ Become involved in doing good things, but with unhealthy motives

V. Suggestions for what to do with my Inner Room

- Identify when I am heading to the Inner Room or recognize when I am already there.
- Speak out loud, "I'm choosing to go to my Inner Room." If already there say, "I'm choosing to stay in my Inner Room."
- Some questions to ask myself while I'm there:
  - Does coming to this place help?
  - How much of my life is controlled by this place?
  - Is there another way of living that is free from this place?
- Gradually, choices can be made to exit the room quickly, or not to go there at all.

Freedom from the Inner Room comes when I realize what the Redeemer wants to do with the ingredients in this place.

Appendix D: Ephesians 1-5

Larry R. Wagner, Ph.D. 2015

My identity is determined by who I am in Christ

Ephesians 1

1. I have the title of saint (v. 1)
2. I am described as the faithful in Christ Jesus (v. 1)
3. My greetings are marked by an extension of grace and peace (v. 2)
4. I am blessed with spiritual blessings (v. 3)
5. I am chosen / pursued (v. 4)
6. I was known before the creation of the world (v. 4)
7. I am holy and blameless in His sight (v. 4)
8. I am the recipient of His love (v. 4)
9. I am adopted into God's family (v. 5)
10. I am the beneficiary of Jesus' work (v. 5)
11. I am the object of His pleasure (v. 5)
12. I am the recipient of His glorious grace (v. 6)
13. I have redemption through His blood (v. 7)
14. I receive forgiveness for my sins (v. 7)
15. I get to experience the riches of God's grace (v. 7)
16. I am given what I need to understand what this means (v. 8)
17. I am the one He delights to show the mystery of His will (v. 9)
18. I am brought into unity with all His creation under His headship (v. 10)
19. I am chosen to be an integral part of His plan (v. 11)
20. I am a source of praise for His glory (v. 12)
21. I am included in Christ (v. 13)
22. I am the recipient of truth that leads to salvation (v. 13)

23. I am one who believes (v. 13)
24. I am a marked man – sealed with the Holy Spirit (v. 13)
25. I have a guaranteed inheritance (v. 14)
26. I am His possession and will therefore experience a final act of glorious redemption at His return (v. 14)
27. I am known as one who lives by faith (v. 15)
28. I am known as one who loves others (v. 15)
29. I am an encouragement to others (v. 16)
30. I am to be upheld by the prayers of my companions (v. 16)
31. I am invited to receive the Holy Spirit's gift of wisdom and insight into knowing God better (v. 17)
32. I also am invited to experience a spiritual enlightenment so that I may know:
   - the hope I have in Christ
   - the riches of His glorious inheritance and
   - the incomparably great power that is at work within me as a believer, the same power that raised Christ from the dead and seated Him at His place of total authority (v. 18 – 23)

Ephesians 2

33. I was dead in my transgressions and sins (v. 1)
34. I lived according to the ways of this world (v. 2)
35. I was under the influence of the ruler of this world (v. 2)
36. I threw my energies toward gratifying the cravings of my old nature (v. 3)
37. I followed the desires and thoughts of my old nature (v. 3)
38. I was by nature an object of wrath (v. 3)
39. I am the recipient of His great love (v. 4)
40. I am the recipient of His rich mercy (v. 4)
41. I was taken off death row and given a completely new life in Christ (v. 5)
42. I am the recipient of a total work of grace (v. 5)

43. I am raised up with Christ so that I may enjoy life from an eternal perspective (v. 6)

44. I have a front row seat to watch and experience the incomparable riches of His grace being poured out (v. 7)

45. I am the recipient of His kindness as expressed through Christ Jesus (v. 7)

46. I am the recipient of a gift (faith) so that I may receive another gift (salvation) (v. 8)

47. I recognize that I did nothing to deserve or earn this gift of salvation (v. 9)

48. I am God's workmanship (v. 10)

49. I am created in Christ Jesus to do good works (v. 10)

50. I am invited to walk into what has already been prepared for me to do (v. 10)

51. I used to be separate from Christ (v. 11 & 12)

52. I used to be without hope (v. 12)

53. I used to be without God (v.12)

54. I am now brought near by the blood of Christ (v. 13)

55. I am the recipient of His peace (v. 14)

56. I am a follower of the One who destroys barriers of hostility (v. 14)

57. I am free from the law with its commandments and regulations because of Christ's sacrifice (v. 15)

58. I am part of a master plan that brings all people together in Christ (v. 15 & 16)

59. I am invited to live a life of peace with all believers regardless of whether they grew up in the church or lived opposed to the teachings of Christ (v. 17)

60. I have access to the Father through the Spirit (v. 18)

61. I am a member of God's household – a household that has Christ Jesus as the chief cornerstone (v. 19 & 20)

62. I am joined with all other believers in Christ to become a dwelling place where God lives by His Spirit (v. 21 & 22)

Ephesians 3

63. I am a prisoner of Christ Jesus for the sake of others (v. 1)
64. I take what Christ pours into me and release it into the lives of others (v. 2)
65. I am invited to have insight into the mystery of Christ (v. 4)
66. I am one of the means the Holy Spirit uses to reveal God's plan to others (v. 5)
67. I am connected with all believers to share in the promise of Christ Jesus (v. 6)
68. I am a servant of the gospel (v. 7)
69. I am the recipient of the gift of God's grace (v. 7)
70. I have God's power working in me (v. 7)
71. I am totally undeserving of the grace given to me (v. 8)
72. I proclaim the Good News (unsearchable riches) of Christ to those who have not heard (v. 8)
73. I give people a clear message of the Creator's eternal purpose that was accomplished in Christ Jesus our Lord (v. 9 – 11)
74. I am in Christ (v. 12)
75. I have faith in Him that allows me to approach God with confidence and freedom (v. 12)
76. I am willing to do whatever it takes to get the message of God's plan in Christ out to those who need it (v.13)
77. I kneel before the Father on behalf of those I serve (v. 14)
78. I am given family name of my Father (v. 15)
79. I pray for those I serve that out of His glorious riches 1) He may strengthen them with power, 2) through His Spirit, 3) in their inner being (v. 16)
80. I long for Christ to dwell in their hearts through faith (v. 17)
81. I pray that they will be rooted and established in love (v. 17)
82. I pray that they will have power to grasp how wide and long and high and deep is the love of Christ (v. 18)
83. I pray that they will know this love that surpasses knowledge (v. 19)

84. I pray that they will be filled to the measure of all the fullness of God (v. 19)
85. I am in relationship with the One who is able to do immeasurably more than all we ask or imagine (v. 20)
86. I am the recipient of this power at work in me (v. 20)
87. I celebrate His glory in the church and in Christ Jesus for all generations throughout eternity (v. 21)

Ephesians 4

88. I am a prisoner for the Lord (v. 1)
89. I am to live a life worthy of the calling I've received (v. 1)
90. I am to be completely humble (v. 2)
91. I am to be gentle (v. 2.)
92. I am to be patient, bearing with others in love (v. 2)
93. I make every effort to keep the unity of the Spirit through the bond of peace (v. 3)
94. I believe that there is one true body of Christ that is held together by the one Spirit (v. 4.)
95. I am called to one hope (v. 4)
96. I believe in one Lord, one faith, and one baptism (v. 5)
97. I believe in one God and Father, who is over all, through all, and in all (v. 6)
98. I am the recipient of grace as Christ apportioned it (v. 7)
99. I am the recipient of specific spiritual gifts (v. 8 – 11)
100. I am to use my gifts as a means to prepare God's people for works of service (v. 12)
101. I have an important role in building up the body of Christ (v. 12)
102. I desire to have unity in the faith and in the knowledge of the Son of God (v. 13)
103. I am to become mature, attaining to the full measure of Christ (v. 13)

104. I am no longer an infant in my faith who is easily deceived by false teaching and deceitful schemes (v. 14)
105. I speak the truth in love (v. 15)
106. I am becoming more like Christ in all areas of my life (v. 15)
107. I receive the life-giving power of Christ flowing through me and joining with others as His body grows (v. 16)
108. I am no longer under the influence of futile thinking (v. 17)
109. I allow my heart to become sensitive to the Spirit's work in order to gain insight into the ways of God (v. 18)
110. I am sensitive to the work of the Spirit so that my old nature and its cravings are held in check (v. 19)
111. I live in a manner that is consistent with the truth I know about Jesus (v. 20, 21)
112. I put off my old self and its corrupted, deceitful desires (v. 22)
113. I am made new in the attitude of my mind (v. 23)
114. I put on a new self which is created to be like God in righteousness and holiness (v. 24)
115. I put off falsehood (v. 25)
116. I speak truthfully to my neighbor (v. 25)
117. I am one of many members of the body (v. 25)
118. I become angry, but do not let it lead me into sin (v. 26)
119. I am dedicated to making quick recoveries (v. 26)
120. I do not let unresolved issues become a staging ground for the enemy (v. 27)
121. I have a work ethic that prevents me from falling into sin (v. 28)
122. I am always aware of how I can use the blessings God gives me to benefit others (v. 28)
123. I do not let any unwholesome talk come from my mouth (v. 29)
124. I only speak what is helpful for building others up (v. 29)
125. I speak in a way that benefits those who are listening (v. 29)
126. I do nothing that would grieve the Holy Spirit (v. 30)
127. I am sealed by the Holy Spirit for the day of redemption (v. 30)

128. I get rid of the junk in my heart – bitterness, rage, anger, brawling, slander, and every form of malice (v. 31)
129. I am kind and compassionate to others (v. 32)
130. I forgive others (v. 32)
131. I receive what Christ did to reunite me with God the Father (v. 32)

Ephesians 5

132. I study the ways of God and then imitate them (v. 1)
133. I am a dearly loved child of God (v. 1)
134. I live a life of love (v. 2)
135. I love others as Christ loved me (v. 2)
136. I give my life up for others (v. 2)
137. I live my life as a sacrifice to God (v. 2)
138. I do not entertain even a hint of sexual immorality, impurity, or greed (v. 3)
139. I am one of God's holy people (v. 3)
140. I speak without using obscenities, foolish talk, or coarse joking (v. 4)
141. I speak with expressions of thanksgiving (v. 4)
142. I do not use people, religion, or things for my purposes (v. 5)
143. I am not deceived by religious smooth talk (v. 6)
144. I avoid being influenced by people who are full of religious sales talk, but want nothing to do with following God (v. 6, 7)
145. I have gone from living in the darkness to living in the light of Christ (v. 8)
146. I live in the light – the fruit that grows from this light is marked by goodness, righteousness, and truth (v. 9)
147. I enjoy finding ways to please Jesus (v. 10)
148. I have nothing to do with the fruitless deeds of darkness, in fact I expose them (v. 11)
149. I am no longer associated with those who carry out their sinful ways in secret (v. 12)

150. I want the light of Christ to make His deep work in my heart transparent to all (v. 13, 14)
151. I am careful in how I live (v. 15)
152. I live as one who is wise (v. 15)
153. I am on the offense making the most of every opportunity (v. 16)
154. I am no longer governed by foolishness (v. 17)
155. I focus my best energies on God's agenda (v. 17)
156. I do nothing that will compromise my availability to do the work of Christ (v. 18)
157. I am continuously being filled with the Holy Spirit (v. 18)
158. I speak to others from a heart that is overflowing with songs of praise to God (v. 19)
159. I have a heart that is so in tune with God's presence that it naturally responds to Him in praise (v. 19)
160. I acknowledge as often as possible my gratitude for all that God does for me, especially giving me the gift of Jesus (v. 20)
161. I submit to others out of reverence for Christ (v. 21)

Appendix E: I-We Overlap

Larry R. Wagner, Ph.D. 2015

Variations of I/We overlap

A.

Balanced

B.

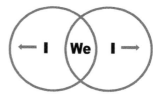

Roommates

C.

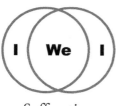

Suffocating

D.

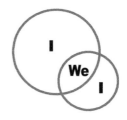

Needing, not Loving

E.

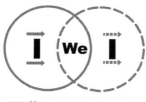

Willing I, Resistant I

Appendix F: The Critical Pause

Larry R. Wagner, Ph.D. 2015

Key Verses that Discuss Conflict

Prov. 15:1   A gentle answer turns away wrath, but a harsh word stirs up anger.

Luke 6:45   Out of the overflow of the heart the mouth speaks.

Eph. 4:26   Be angry, but do not sin.

James 1:19   Let every one of you be quick to hear, slow to speak, and slow to anger.

The Critical Pause

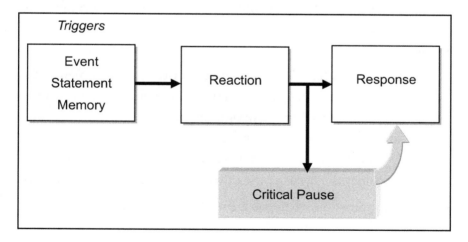

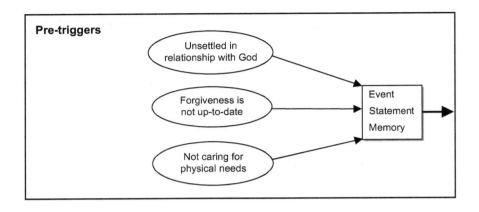

Guidelines for How to Use the Critical Pause

A. How do you enter the CP?

   1. Let the other person know you need some time to regroup. If you stop talking or walk away without communication, you are probably treating yourself to a good pout.

   2. Set a time when you think you will be ready to resume the discussion.

B. What do you do while in the CP?

   1. Seek God's help in generating an attitude readjustment. This includes accepting personal responsibility for whatever part you may have played in the disagreement.

   2. Identify the needs you have that are not being met.

   3. Consider how to express these needs in a healthy manner.

   4. Consider the needs of the other person that are not being met.

C. How do you know when you are ready to exit the Critical Pause and resume the discussion?

   1. When you are no longer interested in who is right or in how to win the argument.

   2. When you can say to yourself, "As a result of the upcoming discussion, I want us to be closer."

Appendix G: The Forgiveness Marker

Larry R. Wagner, Ph.D. 2015

The Forgiveness Marker

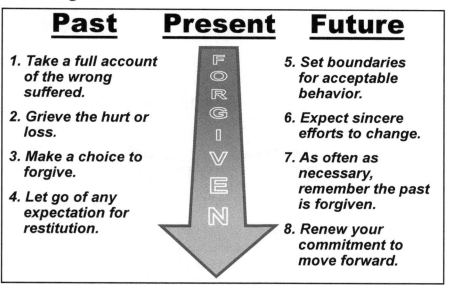

Past   **Present**   **Future**

1. Take a full account of the wrong suffered.

2. Grieve the hurt or loss.

3. Make a choice to forgive.

4. Let go of any expectation for restitution.

5. Set boundaries for acceptable behavior.

6. Expect sincere efforts to change.

7. As often as necessary, remember the past is forgiven.

8. Renew your commitment to move forward.

CONTACT INFORMATION

To order additional copies of this book, please visit
www.redemption-press.com.
Also available on Amazon.com and BarnesandNoble.com
Or by calling toll free 1-844-2REDEEM.

CPSIA information can be obtained
at www.ICGtesting.com
Printed in the USA
BVHW040148201219
567305BV00018B/84/P